Alexander Williamson

Fig. 1 Portrait of Alexander Williamson by John Collier. Courtesy of the Department of Chemistry, UCL.

Alexander Williamson

*A Victorian chemist and the making
of modern Japan*

Takaaki Inuzuka
Translated by Haruko Laurie

Acknowledgements

UCL Press and the contributors to this publication are grateful for the invaluable assistance of Professor William Brock in the preparation of this English edition of the book.

First published in 2021 by
UCL Press
University College London
Gower Street
London WC1E 6BT

Available to download free: www.uclpress.co.uk

ISBN: 978-1-78735-933-8 (Hbk.)
ISBN: 978-1-78735-932-1 (Pbk.)
ISBN: 978-1-78735-931-4 (PDF)
ISBN: 978-1-78735-934-5 (epub)
ISBN: 978-1-78735-935-2 (mobi)
DOI: https://doi.org/10.14324/111.9781787359314

Contents

List of figures

Foreword

This translation into English of Professor Inuzuka's ground-breaking work, which is owed to Mrs Haruko Uryu Laurie, a Fellow of Selwyn College in the University of Cambridge, who for 30 years taught Japanese in the Faculty of Asian and Middle Eastern Studies, is notable for two things. The first is its extreme accuracy in relation to the original text, and the second is the excellency of the English in which it is written.

This being said, those readers fluent in both languages and familiar with both texts may be somewhat puzzled by the fact that the two texts do indeed diverge in certain ways, and this is the reason for the decision to add this foreword to the English edition.

The main problem for English-speaking readers is with the usage of personal names. There was in the first place the well-known fact that, as is still the case, what in English is called the surname always comes last when more than one name is given, whereas in Japanese it comes first, while when only one name of a given person appears in a formal English text, it is normally the surname that is used.

However, the vast majority of English speakers are probably unaware that in mid-nineteenth-century Japan many people used two or more completely different names in the course of their lives, sometimes in sequence and sometimes all at the same time, in accord with the varying purposes for which they were being used. Professor Inuzuka, thinking in terms of a Japanese readership, whom he also assumed would be thoroughly versed in what happened at a turning point in the history of Japan, saw no need to speak of such things.

The result for many English speakers – who have never even heard of most of the students who came to UCL in 1863 and 1865 until they read this book – is that the two chapters that focus on them would become a kaleidoscope of names, popping in and out of existence. This took a good deal of sorting out before it made sense.

To clarify things and make reading easier, all the Japanese names follow the English practice and the names of the students are exactly the same as those carved on the monument in UCL in 1993, while any assumed names follow in brackets, except in one or two cases in which an assumed name was retained by the student concerned as his permanent, main name.

Apart from this, the principal changes to the original Japanese text are emendations of three sentences concerned with the actual history of the making of the monument in UCL and of that in Brookwood Cemetery unveiled in 2013.

In the course of preparing the English edition for publication, Professor Alwyn Davies, former head of the UCL Chemistry Department, a tower of strength beside Kemmyo Taira Sato from the very start of the project, pointed out that Professor Inuzuka had not set out to write a sort of *omnium gatherum* of events in the late nineteenth century, but had concentrated on the heart of his biography, the achievements of Professor Williamson himself and his amazing encounter with the Japanese pioneers, who had suddenly arrived in England in 1863 and 1865, with the result that there is virtually no mention of their subsequent careers. It was therefore decided that an afterword, giving the briefest of indications of every student's subsequent achievements and activities, should be added to the English edition in order to give some idea of the full impact of the story that Professor Inuzuka has told so well.

Historians sometimes talk a little glibly of turning points and revolutions, but in this case both the terms are apt. The Meiji Restoration in 1868 was in itself a revolution, marking the end of Japan's centuries-old traditions of political and social governance. The rapid evolution of a new system to replace it was indeed a turning point, since it marks the birth of Japan as a modern nation and makes a radical turn from isolation to involvement in world affairs. The latter immediately transformed not only the relationship between Britain and Japan, but also that between Japan and all the other major Western powers.

Only a swift glance at the afterword is required to show how quite extraordinary the part played by a handful of Japanese students eventually became. One of them was four times the prime minister of the new Japan; another rose to be minister of foreign affairs. The first director of the Japanese Railway Board was among them, as was the first director of the mint, the secretary of state in the Ministry of Industries, the first minister of education, and the man whose many-faceted entrepreneurial activities laid the foundations for the modern city of Osaka; the list goes on and on.

Nothing of all of this could possibly have been foreseen by anyone when those first students came to UCL, and in its own way, it is a tribute to a great man that his biography has been written by a Japanese historian.

In short, this is indeed a book which anyone who is interested in Anglo-Japanese relations certainly should read. It is also an outstanding tribute to Professor Inuzuka's courage and tenacity, as well as his scholarship, that he managed to complete his great work so swiftly, before finally succumbing to a terminal illness and dying on 22 March 2020.

John White
Former head of the Department of History of Art and Honorary Fellow, UCL

Preface

About 40 years ago when I was doing research on the young Japanese men who went to London during the second half of the nineteenth century I came across the name Alexander William Williamson, who was a distinguished British chemist. I remember very well how I was drawn to the words used to describe him in the *Dictionary of National Biography*: 'Owing to Williamson's scientific influence, force of character, and cosmopolitan outlook, he was chosen guardian of a small group of young Japanese noblemen who came to England in 1863 …'

I have mentioned Williamson's name in several of my books and papers without giving proper consideration to those words, and recently I was given an opportunity to look at his life in more detail and I realised how great this man was. I came to understand what expressions such as 'scientific influence', 'force of character' and 'cosmopolitan outlook' really meant. I also realised the enormity of his contribution to Japan. His influence went well beyond the world of science and it helped to shape ideas and ideals at the time of Japan's modernisation. Many of the young men who studied under Williamson went on to major roles in modernising the country, and Williamson's teaching and his 'cosmopolitan outlook' were fundamental to their creative thinking.

In order to explain his 'cosmopolitan outlook' more precisely, I formulated the expression 'unity out of difference' from the title of Williamson's inaugural lecture at UCL, 'Development of Difference, the Basis of Unity' as I thought this was the key concept for understanding his life. I would like to emphasise that this 'unity out of difference' refers not only to the academic world of science but also to all human activities and endeavours.

I wanted to write about how the young Japanese who were influenced by Williamson lived. They did not simply bring Williamson's work back with them; they also examined and re-examined what they had learned from him and tried to get it to take root in Japan in a form that was suitable for the country's culture and circumstances. This was no easy task: they went through agonising times and some shortened their lives in the process. It took time and tremendous effort to establish the idea of 'unity out of difference' in Japan, and I would be very happy if this book helps readers to sense what these young Japanese men went through.

It was perhaps a foolhardy exploit for me to take on the task of writing the biography of a chemist as I am familiar with neither science nor its history. I decided, nevertheless, to take on the challenge because Williamson's life had such far-reaching consequences for Japan's modern history. I consulted a large number of primary and secondary sources and went through a long process in terms of both selection and interpretation. I have tried my best, but scientists may well find errors and unclear parts. I seek the candid criticism of my readers.

May 2015

1
A traveller of intelligence

Wandsworth, now an inner London borough, was once a picturesque town on the river Thames about four miles southwest of London. In the eighteenth century it was a parish in Surrey, and the gentle rural landscape was scattered with estates owned by nobles and gentry, such as the Archbishop of York and Earl Spencer. Windmills were dotted here and there and the sound of milling never ceased. After the industrial revolution the windmills were replaced by modern flourmill factories, but the peaceful landscape with its grazing cows remained untouched. The River Wandle flowed gently northwards across the fields to the Thames.

Residential areas were developed on the left bank of the Wandle, the town hall and hotels were built during the nineteenth century, and the population increased. On late Victorian maps you can find names such as 'Wandle Terrace', which suggests a residential area.

Alexander Williamson senior

On 10 July 1820 in a small church in this beautiful town, a young man from Elgin, Scotland, married a daughter of a merchant and fellow countryman, William McAndrew. The young man was Alexander Williamson and the bride's name was Antonia McAndrew; they were both 34 years old. Alexander was a young man with hopes and dreams. His grandfather had been a very successful Elgin merchant dealing in gloves, and his father had come to London and taken up a job as a clerk in the East India Company. Alexander was the fourth of nine children. He was lucky to have an opportunity to work for the Company, following in his father's footsteps and those of his godfather and maternal uncle, Alexander Gray, who was a well-known doctor working for the Company in Calcutta. Alexander Gray later founded Dr Gray's Hospital in Elgin.

Alexander Williamson senior was a strong-willed young man with a quick and ingenious mind. It did not take long for him to be noticed by his seniors in the East India Company, and his direct superior, James Mill (1773–1836), took him under his wing. Mill was a high-flyer in the Communications Section of the Company, but he was better known in Britain and abroad as a social thinker. A graduate of Edinburgh University, Mill met the utilitarian Jeremy Bentham (1748–1832) in 1808, and became both friend and disciple, helping to spread Bentham's philosophy and establish the 'Philosophical Radical' movement.

Williamson senior respected Mill as if he were an elder brother, and was clearly influenced significantly by utilitarianism. Mill's thought was rooted in moral philosophy, which aimed to make sense of politics, economics, law and culture from the point of view of human nature, tracing social development according to a set of rules. His wife Antonia was well aware of her husband's nature and gave him unfailing support. She seems to have been an attractive woman with a strong will and great intelligence, and was loved by many. While in Wandsworth the couple were blessed with two children, Antonia Helen (1823–1896), named after her mother and her father's sister, and Alexander William (1824–1904), named after his father and grandfather. The Williamsons hoped their children's lives would be happy and fulfilled.

Cheerful voices in Park Gate House

In 1825, a year after their son's birth, thinking of the health of his wife and children, Williamson senior bought a large house with its own grounds near Brighton, 50 miles south of London (Fig. 2.). He installed the family there and came to see them frequently from London. It was not until 1841 that the railway between London and Brighton was opened, so he travelled by coach. The house, Park Gate House, was in the small village of Ringmer, near Lewes, to the northeast of Brighton, and stands there still today, a typical Georgian-style house with a beautifully symmetrical front, set in green surroundings.

Soon after they moved James (1826–1833) was born. Alex was very happy to have a younger brother. Park Gate House was always filled with children's voices and Williamson senior took great pleasure in going to see his family from London. The only worry Williamson senior had was his eldest son Alex's health. From his birth he was delicate and sickly.

Fig. 2   Park Gate House. Courtesy of Taira Sato.

Alexander and Antonia hoped that Alex would grow strong, and he was fed with donkey's milk for a while as it was believed to be similar to human milk and very nutritious.

It was Alex's eyes that caused him the most serious problems. Both his doctor and his parents were so concerned about a recurring eye infection that they failed to realise that he was generally unhealthy. It was not until Alex was 16 that his doctor recognised the importance of improving his general health. He ended up losing the sight in his right eye, and he also lost full use of his left arm, possibly due to it being bandaged for too long to cover an abscess. Despite these difficulties, he managed to establish himself in the academic world. This was testament to his strength of character, but also thanks to the unfailing support and encouragement of his sister Helen. George Carey Foster, who worked under Alex at the University of London in later years and became a professor of physics, wrote about Helen as follows:

> She combined admirable accomplishments with much force of character, and intellectual independence with great kindness of heart. She was untiring in acts of well-considered and persevering benevolence. Although this lady's career forms no part of the subject of this notice, her qualities of heart and mind are not without interest as throwing an indirect light on the moral and

intellectual characteristics of the home in which she and her illustrious brother grew up.[1]

Words like 'well-considered', 'untiring in acts' and 'benevolence', used here to describe Helen, were also apt descriptions for Alex.

The establishment of UCL

In 1831 Williamson senior purchased a large house with a garden in Wright's Lane in Kensington and moved his family back to London. The house was situated in a quiet residential area on the south side of Kensington Gardens, only seven or eight minutes' walk from Kensington Palace. He chose this area because the family of James Mill, for whom he had such great respect, lived nearby.

In 1826, five years before this move, Williamson senior had made an offer of financial support in aid of an educational project planned by James Mill and the 'philosophical radicals', namely to establish a university within London itself.

The initial idea for creating a new institute for higher education came from a Glasgow-born poet, Thomas Campbell (1777–1844), who was also an ally of Bentham. He approached Lord Henry Brougham (1778–1868), a statesman who shared the same beliefs, advocating the necessity of establishing an institute of higher learning in London for the middle classes, for effectively and multifariously teaching, examining, exercising and rewarding with honours, in the liberal arts and sciences.

Lord Brougham, who had helped to found an influential magazine, the *Edinburgh Review*, responded immediately and started raising money by asking liberals and utilitarians for their help. James Mill was also involved in this effort of founding a new university and worked tirelessly at fundraising. Williamson senior, who was Mill's friend and shared his views on education, became a major contributor.

Preparations for establishing a University of London went smoothly. A ceremony to lay the foundation stone at Gower Street, where the university would be located, took place on 30 April 1827 and construction work began thereafter. It took one and a half years for the building to be completed, and lectures started on 1 October 1828 (Fig. 3). The University of London was created in response to the wishes of a bourgeois middle class, and the core founders were utilitarian and liberal educationalists. Unlike the more traditional universities of Oxford and Cambridge, London was to be open to people of all faiths, and its distinct

Fig. 3   UCL in *c*. 1828. Courtesy of UCL Special Collections.

characteristic was to be its teaching of practical sciences and technology in response to the demands of the time. It was an institution well suited to an age of 'progress' and 'sciences and technology', symbols of nineteenth-century European civilisation after the industrial revolution. When King's College, affiliated with the Church of England, was established, the name of the university was changed to University College, and in 1836 both institutions came together to form the University of London. They would play a significant role in modern higher education in the United Kingdom.

Father's wish

Williamson senior would often visit James Mill's house and they had many discussions on religious, social and educational issues. James's son, John Stuart Mill (1806–1873), who later became the most prominent utilitarian thinker of the nineteenth century, was also studying under his father's guidance. Then in his twenties, John Stuart Mill was a most gifted young man. While working for the East India Company as a clerk like his father, he published some papers in the *Edinburgh Review* that attracted considerable attention among the philosophical radicals. It is probable that, having formed a good relationship with the young Mill,

Williamson senior asked him for advice regarding Alex's education. He had lost his second son James to illness in 1833, so all his hopes and aspirations naturally fell on the first born, Alex. Years later, in 1887, Alex looked back on this period and remembered:

> When I was a small boy, I was once walking with my father in some fields northward – in what is now Gordon Square. I do not know what my age was, but I know that there was a paling about *so* high, and I could just look over it, so I don't suppose that I was very old. A dome was visible; I could see it across the palings. I was told 'That is London University, and when you are old enough you will go and study there.' My father was one of those who originally contributed money towards the building of it. My father did not at that time know how fully his wish would be realized for I have been a student here, I believe I may say in the best sense of the word, although my student career began by my appointment as Professor of Practical Chemistry.[2]

The reason that Williamson senior decided to move his family back to London in 1831 was perhaps because his son Alex had reached school age. Seven years later he suddenly resigned his post at the East India Company, soon after Alex started to attend Kensington Grammar School. Williamson senior was 52 years old. He had looked up to James Mill as a father or elder brother, and Mill's death in 1836 may well have been the reason for his resignation. Persuaded by John Stuart Mill, who had lived in Paris, to visit France, he decided to take the whole family to Paris. John Stuart Mill was at that time deeply absorbed in Henri de Saint-Simon's (1760–1825) philosophy of history and socialism in France, as well as Auguste Comte's (1798–1857) positivism, particularly after reading the second volume of Comte's *Cours de philosophie positive* (published in 1835). Comte was originally a mathematician, but advocated positivism in the field of philosophy to overcome the crises in society after the French Revolution, and by doing so he established sociology as a discipline. For Comte, civilisation had proceeded through three stages – a theological stage in which natural phenomena and man's place in nature were explained as the result of supernatural or divine powers, a metaphysical stage with a more enlightened view that sought explanations in terms of natural material powers, and a third scientific or positive stage in which natural phenomena were explained by experimentally tested facts and subsumed within general laws and theories. He also had an interest in education. He considered that the positivist approach in teaching and the education system would be a potent tool for social and political reorganisation. In later years Alex would become deeply influenced by Comte's philosophy.

A dream born in Heidelberg

From Paris the Williamsons moved to Dijon, in southeast France, and Alex attended college there. He then started spending winter months in the city of Wiesbaden, 250 miles away from Dijon, to study German. Wiesbaden had a mild climate and was well known as a spa resort. Alex's German improved considerably while he was there and it is thought that it was probably around this time that he started to show an interest in becoming a chemist. In 1840, at the age of 16, Alex entered the University of Heidelberg. The oldest university in Germany, Heidelberg was established in 1386, and was known as a humanistic institution of higher education during the Reformation in the sixteenth century. It subsequently experienced a difficult period and was nearly closed down, but after 1803, when Heidelberg became a part of the region of Baden, it was re-established and began to flourish, producing such philosophers as Wilhelm Windelband and G.W.F. Hegel.

Following his father's wishes, Alex went to Heidelberg to study medicine. He studied anatomy under Friedrich Tiedemann (1781–1861) and chemistry under Leopold Gmelin (1788–1853). He found Tiedemann's lectures tedious and uninspiring, but was enthused by Gmelin's teaching, in particular the extra classes he offered in his own laboratory. Alex was fascinated by his experiments and became a frequent visitor to Gmelin's laboratory. Gmelin was known for his attempt to systematise chemical theory using the concept of chemical equivalent, and his name survives in 'Gmelin's test', which is still used today to diagnose liver diseases.

Gmelin gave kind guidance to Alex but was totally against his idea of giving up medicine and becoming a chemist. He argued that it would be extremely difficult for someone with Alex's disabilities – the problems with his eyes and arm – to succeed as a chemist. Alex, however, turned a deaf ear to his teacher's advice. When Alex's father learned of his son's intentions he was also strongly opposed. For Williamson senior, the term 'chemist' meant nothing but shop windows with shining glass bottles; he misunderstood the term 'chemist' and thought his son intended to be a dispenser or a pharmacist. 'Chemistry' as a science was not widely understood by the public in the Britain of the time. It was the Irish aristocrat Robert Boyle (1627–1691) who elevated its status to one of the pure sciences. Before Boyle chemistry was not regarded as a proper 'science'. Chemistry had been closely associated with alchemy from the Middle Ages but Boyle, in his book *The Sceptical Chymist* (1661), moved it into the realm of science by introducing modern experimental methods. He encouraged chemical research based on strictly controlled experiments in the same way as astronomers and physicists were carrying out their work, and he argued that chemistry should be an independent subject in natural sciences and that its aim should be to unlock parts of the mystery of the universe and to seek truth for the sake of truth.

Boyle was one of the founders of the Royal Society. In 1645 a number of young scientists, including Boyle, formed the 'Invisible College', which became the core of a formal academic group in 1660. It received royal approval two years later to become the Royal Society. Members are known as 'Fellows', and there were 55 Fellows at the time of its foundation. Boyle was asked to be the President of the Royal Society in 1680 but he declined and conceded the honour to Sir Christopher Wren. He died in 1691, having devoted his entire life to chemistry in its early days.

But we have digressed.

Even in the nineteenth century, in England chemists did not enjoy a high status, so Alex's father was still concerned about his son's choice of subject. But much to his father's unease, Alex was totally committed to his research in chemistry. He created a private laboratory in his house in Heidelberg and devoured every chemistry book he could lay his hands on. Gmelin soon recognised Alex's true enthusiasm and ability, and tried to persuade his family to accept his desire to be a chemist, writing to Alex's mother, Antonia, to say her son would certainly be a chemist.[3] Alex's father reluctantly agreed, bowed to Gmelin's word and gave his permission. In later years when Alex reminisced, he never failed to mention Gmelin, commenting that 'I had the good fortune to obtain an unusual degree of personal kindness and instruction from that distinguished chemist'.[4]

Professor Liebig's laboratory

Having graduated from Heidelberg University, Alex, on Gmelin's recommendation, moved to Giessen, then the Mecca of research in chemistry. This old town, in the state of Hessen, is located at an important crossroads about 35 miles north of Frankfurt. The university was established in 1607 in the centre of the town. Its reputation was due to the presence of Justus von Liebig, the Professor of Chemistry. He was elected as professor at the young age of 21, and he initiated a completely new method of teaching chemistry, which was to instruct students through practical experiments. Students first of all studied quantitative and qualitative analysis, followed by experiments analysing organic compounds; only then were they given their own topic of research. Liebig pioneered the new field of organic chemistry and was instrumental in its rapid progress. His reputation spread not only in Germany but also all over Europe, America and beyond. Various German dialects as well as many European languages were heard in his laboratory. Even in Britain, where there was very little interest in chemistry at the time, Liebig's name was well known.[5]

Liebig went to Britain in 1837 and gave several lectures, which encouraged some to engage with his work. He discussed the importance of chemistry for agriculture and industry, and in Britain, then in the midst of an industrial revolution, his chemistry started to draw the attention of the rising bourgeoisie. With the support and sponsorship of Prince Albert, who was keen to promote science education, the Royal College of Chemistry was established in 1845, and the first president was one of Liebig's leading pupils, August Wilhelm von Hofmann (1818–1892).

Four years previously, in 1841, Thomas Graham (1805–1869), Professor in Chemistry at UCL, had laid the foundation for the promotion of chemistry in Britain by establishing the Chemical Society. Graham was from Glasgow and was known as a researcher at the interface between physics and chemistry. Having done pioneering work on the diffusion of gases and dissolved molecules in solution, he moved on to research into colloid chemistry. He became a professor at UCL in 1837, the year that Liebig made his first visit to Britain. So, around the time that Alex was in Giessen completing his last research project, chemistry in Britain was finally poised on the threshold of a new era.

At this time many young chemists were arriving at Giessen. Often, like Alex, they were very much attracted by Liebig's 'pleasing manner' and his affectionate human qualities. In later years, Alex wrote with fond memories of

> the most efficient organisation for the promotion of chemistry which had ever existed … A little community of which each member was fired with enthusiasm for learning by the genius of the great master, and of which the best energies were concentrated on the one subject of experimental investigation.[6]

While in Giessen, Alex lodged at the house of Dr Hillenbrand, Professor of Literature at the university. Alex was a very serious student: rising at six every morning, he never missed a single seven o'clock lecture. His only distractions were walking, and occasional picnics and dances with his friends. He had a good voice and took delight in singing with other students. He obviously enjoyed his student life in Giessen and managed to produce many papers. The liberal atmosphere of the research environment in Giessen gave Alex the chance to approach some problems outside the world of chemistry, which led him to challenge his former teacher Gmelin's theory of galvanism, for example. His ground-breaking paper on a general theory of electricity was much praised by Liebig. In addition, he published his first papers on bleaching salts, the nature of ozone and the composition of Prussian blue. Liebig awarded Alex a doctorate in 1845.[7]

Alex's father paid a visit to Giessen around this time and sought Liebig's views on his son's future as a chemist. According to Alex's diary, Liebig's assessment was:

> That my knowledge and practice in chemistry is now sufficient to enable me to conduct any research ... It is only necessary by reading the chemical journals to keep myself in the current of progress of the day. That the great want of the English chemists consisted in the one-sidedness of their acquirements. They are able to analyse a mineral but are not men of general scientific attainments, which in order to teach the application of chemistry to the different arts should be the case.[8]

And he resolved:

> to apply the next year a time to making my knowledge in Physics, Maths, Technology be as complete and *'grundlich'* [thorough] as possible, ceasing for the time to pursue experimental researches in chemistry.[9]

Liebig explained to Alex's father the necessity of general scientific attainments and the importance of a liberal arts education for enriching humanity. Acting upon Liebig's advice, Alex temporarily abandoned experimental chemistry and concentrated on the study of mathematics, physics and literature. Five times a week for his cultural enrichment he attended Professor Hillenbrand's evening lectures on the history of German literature. He found these lectures 'profitably filled up an hour'.[10]

First steps towards atomic theory

After two productive years in Giessen, Alex's next destination was Paris. John Stuart Mill, who had known him since childhood and recognised his talent, strongly advised him that in order to master advanced mathematics the best option would be to go to France and work under Auguste Comte. Having arrived in August 1846 and taken up residence at 8 rue des Francs-Bourgeois, Alex lost no time in going to see Comte at 10 rue Monsieur-le-Prince.

Comte's fame was increasing day by day thanks to the publication of his six-volume *Cours de philosophie positive* (Course in Positive Philosophy) in 1842 and *Discours sur l'esprit du positif* (A General View of Positivism) in 1844. However, at the time that Alex sought his guidance, Comte was still coming to terms with the sudden death of his beloved Clotilde de Vaux and was facing a philosophical turning point. As is well known, her death was a driving factor in Comte starting to advocate a 'Religion of Humanity' in 1847.

Comte classified science into six basic disciplines and ranked them in hierarchical order: mathematics, astronomy, physics, chemistry, biology and sociology. Mathematics was given highest place because it is the most abstract and general, and the most exact, of the sciences. He considered that all basic sciences were a product of human spiritual activities, and each of them progressed through theological, metaphysical and positive stages, so for him the systematisation of the social sciences was essential if the present age was to reach the positivistic stage.

Alex studied mathematics under Comte three times a week, and had many opportunities to discuss and debate with the other students who frequented Comte's apartments. Thus he learned much from Comte's positivism and he began to consider how to reflect these views in both his own chemistry and his ideas about education in general.

Alex then set up a laboratory at his residence in Paris, and succeeded in producing urea and carbonic acid by the direct oxidation of an amide. He reported these results to the Italian Scientific Congress in Venice in 1847. In Paris he also had the great good fortune to meet Auguste Laurent (1807–1853) of Bordeaux University, and Charles Frédéric Gerhardt (1816–1856) from Montpellier, because both these chemists were working on the question of atomic and molecular weight, a basic challenge for chemical structural formulae. It was here that Alex made his first steps towards an atomic theory. He wrote to a friend:

I have been engaged in extensive research, whose object is to elucidate some obscure, though fundamental, chemical phenomena, my views on which were suggested and gradually developed by my former studies.[11]

He does not say exactly what he meant by 'some obscure, though fundamental, chemical phenomena' but it might have been the question of 'the interchange of atoms among neighbouring molecules'.[12] Most chemists at the time accepted John Dalton's static atomic theory that molecules determined the type of matter and the atom explained the composition of elements. However, the existence of the atom was not something chemists could prove by their experiments, and opinions among chemists were divided; some denied its existence but Alex was of one of those who positively supported the idea.

The shoots of positivistic thought

Alex was in Paris during the 1848 Revolution, known as the February Revolution, when King Louis Philippe was overthrown, and on 27 February the Second Republic was born. For a while people in Paris enjoyed a sense of liberation and freedom, but it did not last long and was replaced with a growing sense of dissatisfaction towards the new government. This saw riots staged by workers on 23–26 June, known as the 'June Days uprising'. Many workers were shot dead or arrested by the National Guard. In Paris many buildings and open public spaces were reduced to ruins, and the romantic ambience that once filled the city disappeared. Theatres were closed and artists fell on hard times.

The realist landscape paintings by Millet and Corot of the Barbizon School; the realist novels of Flaubert, influenced by his understanding of positivism; the literature of Balzac, which dealt with man as his theme; and Comte's positive philosophy and sociology – all these came into existence during this chaotic historical period in France. They all shared a sense of crisis that an organic reorganisation of their society was essential. Experiencing life as a student in the midst of these events, Alex's attitude to both the life of the mind and mathematical theory was influenced to an incalculable degree by Comte's method. As he wrote to his father:

If my experience of Comte's superior powers were insufficient to convince you that his lessons were worth their price, John Mill's saying that he 'would prefer him to any man in Europe to finish a scientific education' ought to carry the point.[13]

The move to UCL

Early in 1849, by which time Alex had lived in Paris for almost three years, Thomas Graham of UCL came to Paris and had a meeting with him. Although Alex was only 25 years old, he had already gained a reputation as a talented scholar in the field of organic chemistry and Graham strongly encouraged him to apply for the post of Professor of Analytical and Practical Chemistry at UCL. George Fownes, who had occupied the position since 1845, had died at a young age in January 1849, and the professorship had become vacant. Graham had at one stage been critical of Alex's interpretation of ozone and ever since then Alex had thought of him as an opponent, so he was most appreciative of Graham's suggestion. He acted swiftly and sent a formal letter of application to the Council of UCL on 26 April (Fig. 4). In that letter he wrote:

> Among the results obtained in my laboratory here [Paris], was one which consisted in producing urea and carbonic acid by direct but regulated combustion of amide. This I personally communicated to the Venetian Congress in 1847.
>
> Here I have also had an opportunity of studying the qualities eminently possessed by this people, of systematising and generalising science. A lesson which I hope to be able to apply with advantage to public institution.[14]

He sounded very confident and added at the end that letters of recommendation would be sent from eminent chemists who knew him well. True enough, from the beginning to the middle of May, letters started arriving from Germany, France and Italy. There were at least 17 of them, from the likes of Liebig, Jean-Baptiste Dumas, Gerhardt, Hermann Kopp, Comte, Gmelin, Laurent, Henri Victor Regnault, Théophile-Jules Pelouze and Hofmann. Liebig wrote:

> Williamson gained my especial esteem by his diligence, his pure and warm love of science, his remarkable talents, and his amiable and excellent qualities as a man. During his stay in this place, he was a pupil of the Laboratory here, in which he made himself most thoroughly acquainted with all the requisites for a teacher of

Practical Chemistry ... Dr Williamson is distinguished beyond others by his profound knowledge in Physics and Mathematics, and he has gained, by his later Philosophical studies, the most valuable requisites of a teacher to an extent in which few possess them.[15]

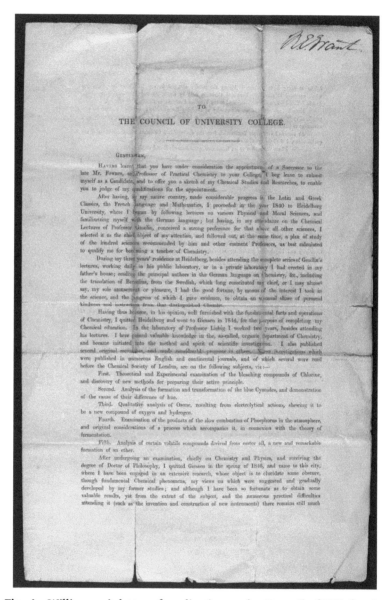

Fig. 4 Williamson's letter of application to the Council of UCL for the Professorship of Practical Chemistry. Courtesy of UCL Special Collections.

Liebig's highest possible praise of Alex was more than enough to convince the Council members of University College. Out of four candidates, Dr John Percy and Alex were shortlisted. While the Council took note of Alex's physical disabilities, they unanimously elected him as their new professor on 16 June. William received official notification of his appointment from the Council on 18 June and he returned to London a week later. He wrote to the Secretary of the Council, Charles C. Atkinson, the same day, expressing how delighted he was to accept the offer: 'I will now start my preparation for the work so that I will not fail your trust placed on me.'[16] Atkinson had served the Council as Secretary since 1835. Alex was overwhelmed with emotion at the thought of a new life at UCL. His father's wish, which he had heard so often in his childhood, had come true.

2
Birkbeck Laboratory at UCL

Alex Williamson left Paris, where the embers of the February Revolution were still smouldering, and returned home in June 1849. After three years in Paris, London appeared prosperous. Just over a decade into the rule of Queen Victoria, the British economy was entering its golden age, and Britain was at the zenith of its prosperity as ruler of the world economy. This was the time now often known as the 'age of steel and coal' or the 'age of the railways', when industrialisation in cities advanced to an unprecedented scale, and a railway network was built to cover the whole country. The new middle class, many of them industrial bourgeoisie, started playing an active role in society.

The whole of London was talking about the Great Exhibition that was to take place in Hyde Park in two years' time and whose patron was no less than Prince Albert. Many industrial goods, produced with the latest scientific technology, were to be exhibited. Williamson must have felt exhilarated to find himself in a London of progress and prosperity.

He initially settled in a house at 15 Holles Place, Hampstead Road. Close to University College and Euston Station, it was a very convenient location. As planned, he became Professor of Analytical and Practical Chemistry, a post within UCL's Faculty of Arts and Laws. He started his lectures on 18 October 1849. Both research and teaching mainly took place in the Birkbeck Laboratory, which was equipped with the newest devices. It had been opened in 1846 and named in honour of Dr George Birkbeck, a physicist and physician, who was a founding member of University College. By combining general chemistry lectures with practicals in the laboratory, students learned to apply chemistry to industrial technology, metallurgy, medicine and agriculture. Williamson's method was designed to discipline students' minds and hands through systematic learning of the theoretical principles of pure chemistry, physics and other sciences, and by practical training in general chemical analysis. This fitted perfectly with middle-class ideas of education in the mid-Victorian era.

When Birkbeck was teaching natural philosophy at the Andersonian Institute (which later became the University of Strathclyde) in Glasgow, he started a low-cost lecture course for workers in response to requests from mechanics who were eager to attain more advanced scientific knowledge. This pioneering educational project led to the establishment of the London Mechanics' Institute in 1823 and played an important role in spreading the sciences to working-class people and the general public. The London Mechanics' Institute later became a part of London University and was known as Birkbeck College, so the Birkbeck Laboratory was a fitting place to realise Birkbeck's desire to popularise science.

The attributes of a teacher

Williamson's inaugural lecture, entitled 'Development of Difference, the Basis of Unity', was given in the Faculty of Arts and Laws on 16 October, prior to the start of his teaching. Many people awaited this unusually titled lecture with considerable interest. He intended to describe European intellectual and social development using the concept of progress, and to conclude that the advancement of civilisation would only be made possible by uniting the diverse cultures of individuals and states. He must have wanted to put forward his own philosophy of 'unity out of difference' in tandem with the educational ethos of University College. The audience expected a lecture on chemistry but instead heard one on sociology. One historian has described the lecture as going down like 'a lead balloon'.[17]

He then began his work. William Augustus Tilden, later Professor of Chemistry at the Royal College of Science, described him as 'a tall, slight and upright figure, arrayed almost uniformly in grey trousers and frock coat; hair and beard grey, with that peculiar look which distinguishes short-sighted people'. And he added:

> He was a splendid teacher, always in the laboratory, going from one student to another, arousing and maintaining their interest in their work, and ready to discuss any point upon which they sought his help … He would never admit that an experimental difficulty was insurmountable; 'If you know clearly', he would say, 'what you want to do, there is always a way of doing it'.[18]

Williamson expected his students to find topics that interested them and to work on them patiently, using new methods. He firmly believed in this approach, and his attitude towards his own research and the way he guided his students remained consistent throughout his life. When the Professor of Theoretical Chemistry, Thomas Graham, was absent Williamson would lecture on general chemistry in his place. Foster, one of his distinguished students, observed that students welcomed him with applause for the reason that 'he seemed to bring out new points of interest in the best-worn subjects by the freshness of his treatment and the new light he would throw on them'.[19]

Theory of etherification

While fully engaged in teaching, Williamson continued his own research at the Birkbeck Laboratory until late every night, and in 1850 he produced his famous theory of etherification. This was read at the British Association in Edinburgh on 3 August, and appeared in the November edition of the *Philosophical Magazine*. A detailed version was published in the *Quarterly Journal of the Chemical Society* two years later.

Williamson distanced himself from the existing theory that ether was formed by loss of water from alcohol, and postulated that it would be possible to produce ether by developing practical methods for preparing homologous higher alcohols. He showed that ether contains two ethyl radicals $[C_2H_5]$ and the same quantity of oxygen as alcohol, and that the relationship between alcohol and ether could not be one of the loss of, or addition of, water. In technical terms, what he did was to prove that in the process of etherification of alcohol there is not loss of water, but the exchange of an ethyl group $[C_2H_5]$ for hydrogen. In other words he discovered that ether $[C_2H_5 \cdot O \cdot C_2H_5]$ is produced by exchanging the $[H]$ from the $[OH]$ of alcohol $[C_2H_5 \cdot OH]$ with ethyl $[C_2H_5]$. This synthetic method of producing ether is named the Williamson synthesis and is known throughout the world even today. It was thus proved that molecules of water, alcohol and ether all contain the same quantity of oxygen. This finding was to lead chemists within a few years to accept that that atomic and molecular weights and formulae had to be based upon Avogadro's Hypothesis that equal volumes of gases at equal pressure and temperature contain the same number of molecules. In addition, by demonstrating that continuous etherification of alcohol by sulphuric acid involved the formation of an intermediate compound, ethyl hydrogen sulphate, Williamson was able to cast doubt on previous explanations of etherification that viewed the acid as a 'catalyst'.

Here he was echoing Comte, for whom 'catalysis' was a metaphysical fancy that had no place in the positive stage that chemistry was striving to achieve. That chemical reactions proceed via chemical intermediates came to play a major role in twentieth-century chemistry. Here Williamson was a pioneer.

The seeds of valency theory

Behind Williamson's theory of etherification lay another important issue, that of atomic theory, which Williamson had been pursuing for many years. The mechanism of etherification was not possible unless it was understood as a process of continuous atomic exchanges, so Williamson began to view atoms and molecules as being in motion, not as the static particles of Dalton's theory. This was the early stage of the theory of 'dynamic atomism'. This theory was not only a step towards the reunification of chemistry with physics, but also became an important driver of research into the unification of organic and inorganic chemistry led by Charles Gerhardt and other scholars.

It was around this time that people began to pay attention to practitioners of organic chemistry. Edward Frankland (1825–1899), professor at Owens College, Manchester, became a particular focus of attention in academic circles when his theory was published in 1852. He was a year younger than Williamson and had also studied under Liebig in Giessen. Through his research work on organometallic compounds he discovered that atoms come together to make chemical compounds in regular ratios, and this theory drew a considerable response. The idea grew from his interest in the similarities of organic and inorganic compounds. 'This was not a clear concept of valence yet but atoms began to be treated as a unit with particular combining force.'[20] One may call this the origin of the 'valence of elements'.

It was a German chemist, Friedrich August Kekulé (1829–1896), who built a foundation of the theory of chemical structure based on Frankland's work. Kekulé was five years younger than Williamson, and his path to becoming a chemist had been unusual. He had entered Giessen University with the intention of studying architecture, but Liebig's lectures had such a powerful influence on him that he changed his mind and decided to become a chemist.

Kekulé came to London in December 1853 to work at St Bartholomew's Hospital as an assistant to John Stenhouse (1809–1880), who had been his senior in Giessen. He often dropped by Williamson's Birkbeck Laboratory on his way home and they would have long discussions until late into the night. They became close friends, and Kekulé always spoke of Williamson with deep affection and respect. He seems to have regarded their association as a significant influence on his own development. Williamson's research room, in a corner of the Birkbeck Laboratory, gradually became a gathering place for young scientists devoted to the 'new type theory' in which organic compounds were classified as the substitution products of four inorganic molecules, hydrogen (H_2), hydrogen chloride (HCl), water (H_2O) and methane (CH_4). Kekulé and William Odling (1829–1921) were often found there and Auguste Laurent and Gerhardt joined them from time to time. It would not be an exaggeration to say that the seeds of valency theory came out of these discussions in Williamson's little research laboratory.

The majesty of the Crystal Palace

British society in the middle of the Victorian era was filled with hopes not only for scientists but also for those who were keen to learn about literature, philosophy, arts, politics and economics, and many people felt that before them stretched unlimited possibilities.

The Great Exhibition, awaited by the entire nation, opened on 1 May 1851 at Hyde Park in London. The huge exhibition hall, designed by the renowned gardener Joseph Paxton, was entirely covered with glass. Its beautiful shape led to it being named the 'Crystal Palace' and it won great acclaim all over Europe. There were 100,000 exhibits and more than six million people visited the exhibition by the closing date of 15 October. These are extraordinary numbers, and the British historian Asa Briggs commented as follows:

> Its purpose was 'to present a true test and living picture of the point of development at which the whole of mankind has arrived ... and a new starting point, from which all nations will be able to direct their further exertions'. In its impressive building and in the wide range of exhibits it offered on display, the Crystal Palace proclaimed triumphantly the visibility of human progress.[21]

The Great Exhibition demonstrated the excellence of British products and industrial technology, and at the same time preached the gospel of work and of peace. The message was that joy and diligence in one's work would lead to world peace, but hidden behind the splendid facade lay poverty, and life remained hard for the general public. Profit from the exhibition was used to build facilities for the arts and sciences, including the Science Museum, in a large area of South Kensington. Promoting further industrialisation, the British government was trying to expand export markets not only within its own colonies but also in under-developed countries in Asia and Central and South America through its free trade policy. This is known as the imperialism of free trade.

The far-reaching impact of 'progress' and 'prosperity'

Britain claimed Hong Kong after her victory in the Opium War in 1842 and began an extensive advance into Asia. A large number of British merchants flooded into East Asia seeking new markets. Many of these, such as James Matheson and William Jardine, built connections with Japan. Riding the wave of increased imports of cotton from India and the opium trade in Asia, they were on their way to establishing powerful commercial enterprises that were to replace the East India Company. Britain entered into diplomatic relations with Japan in October 1854 during the Crimean War against Russia. Jardine, Matheson & Co. opened a branch in Yokohama in 1859, a year after the conclusion of the Anglo-Japanese Treaty of Friendship and Commerce. The company's founder, William Jardine, was a Scot who had worked for the East India Company as a ship's surgeon. Together with James Matheson he set up a trading company dealing with opium between China and India, and importing tea to Britain. This was the beginning of the large enterprise Jardine Matheson, which is still active today. Ripples of the wave of 'progress' and 'prosperity' that Britain triggered at the Great Exhibition thus reached even the shores of Japan, a small country in the Far East, and this wave brought with it a danger of colonisation by great Western powers.

The dawn of a new age

In the world of chemistry at this time, new theories were constantly emerging. Williamson's close friends made significant discoveries that would form the basis of organic chemistry in later years: Gerhardt's 'theory of types' in 1853, and Kekulé's theory of the tetravalence of carbon in 1858. Their contributions towards organic chemistry were so significant that it is generally agreed that the most important work in nineteenth-century organic chemistry was begun by Gerhardt, continued by Williamson and concluded by Kekulé.

The year 1858, when Kekulé's new theory was published, was a huge turning point for Britain. The Government of India Act was passed, the East India Company – which until then had ruled over large swathes of India – was abolished, and India became a united territory directly governed by the India Government Office. The East India Company, which had been a familiar name to Williamson from his childhood, disappeared from the scene, and that year brought the opening of a new age of British imperialism.

Also in this year, Charles Darwin proposed his theory of natural selection, seen by some as the theoretical background to the age of imperialism as the concept of progress through free competition is an underlying idea of industrial capitalism. Called the theory of evolution, it was published in November the following year under the title of *On the Origin of Species*.

Then, borrowing the concept of 'evolution' from Darwin's biological theory of evolution, the philosopher Herbert Spencer advocated a systematic development of social structure. His theory of social evolution was widely accepted in British society as the 'Bible' of 'progress' against the backdrop of scientific advancement and the growth of a middle class. Spencer had published his *Progress: Its Law and Cause* in 1857, the same year that Comte died in poverty in Paris at age of 59.

Emma, his 'better half'

Around this time, as if urged on by the spirit of the age, Williamson was distancing himself from theoretical chemistry and showing more interest in the field of applied chemistry, which is closer to the practical application of science in everyday life.

This change of direction had something to do with his private life. Early in 1854 Williamson became engaged to Emma Catherine Key (Fig. 5, Fig. 6). Emma, born on 18 June 1831, was 23 years old. Her father, Thomas Hewitt Key (1799–1875), was an authority in Latin, and was regarded as the leading figure in British philology. He was Professor of Comparative Grammar at UCL and also Joint Headmaster of University College School, which was within the grounds of UCL. How and when Alex and Emma met and began to be attracted to each other is not known, but they were certainly ideal companions and were happy together throughout their lives. Emma's will (dated 7 March 1913), written 10 years before her death, testifies to their happy marriage.

Fig. 5 Emma Catherine Key (Williamson), 1831–1923. Courtesy of the Williamson collection/Phoebe Barr.

Fig. 6 Alexander Williamson. Courtesy of the Williamson collection/ Phoebe Barr.

The engagement ring Alex gave Emma was a splendid one with two diamonds and three emeralds, and Emma kept it with her throughout her life.

Emma's father was educated at Trinity College, Cambridge and was a member of a group gathered around Thomas Babington Macaulay (1800–1859), a prominent historian and politician. Key was a man of many talents, initially studying medicine and later turning to science and economics. He taught mathematics at the University of Virginia in the US, and was appointed Professor of Classics (Latin) at the newly established UCL in 1828. He became Headmaster of University College School[22] from 1831 and Professor of Comparative Grammar in 1842. He was a great teacher and he was called 'one of the grandest oral teachers of his time'.[23] He had a 'restless and ingenious mind'[24] but he was gentle, and his humble and unassuming attitude, together with his splendid appearance, attracted many students' respect. Emma's passionate but kind and gentle temperament might have come from her father.

Williamson's father was initially unhappy with the engagement because the couple had decided to get engaged without consulting him. An unpleasant atmosphere lingered between father and son for almost a year, but they were reconciled thanks to the intervention of Williamson's mother Antonia. In May 1855, Williamson senior wrote to his wife: 'I am quite reconciled to the engagement and really approve of it'.[25] They finally got married on 1 August 1856, more than a year after Williamson's father had given his approval, a delay due to Williamson's extremely busy life in the university with organisational reform and personnel issues.

In 1855 Thomas Graham, who had been Professor of Theoretical Chemistry at UCL since 1837, was appointed Master of the Mint and left the university. Williamson decided to apply for the Chair of Theoretical Chemistry while retaining his Professorship of Practical and Analytical Chemistry. He had been elected as a Fellow of the Royal Society on 7 June that year (he is depicted among prominent Fellows in a much later image shown here, Fig. 7), and three weeks later, on 30 June, he sent in his application for the post to the Council. To be Professor of Practical Chemistry and Theoretical Chemistry at the same time was unprecedented, but it was his enthusiasm and zeal for combining practical and theoretical chemistry that drove his application. Intensive lobbying of members of the Council, and further testimonies from eminent chemists such as Hofmann, Gerhardt, Robert

Fig. 7 Fellows of the Royal Society, 1885. Wellcome Collection. Williamson is standing on the far right.

Bunsen (1811–1899), Frankland and Stenhouse resulted in the Council unanimously electing him to succeed Graham. He was to hold both chairs for 32 long years until his retirement in 1887.

Chemistry was not the only area Williamson was interested in, and his work started to spread to other fields, including the improvement of stoves for domestic heating, and marine boiler construction. He was enthusiastic about his inventions and discoveries, and even turned his attention to pharmaceutical preparations. Seeing Williamson's slightly unusual behaviour, his father urged him to devote himself exclusively to his professorial duties. Williamson's daughter, Alice Maud Fison, left the following testimony regarding her father's work during this period:

> In his early married life my father had to work so hard for his living (and he and my mother felt it necessary to entertain scientific people a good deal) that he probably had no time or energy left for going on with experimental work. Happy as they undoubtedly were, my mother sometimes remarked to me in later years that perhaps had he remained single he would have gone on with great original work.[26]

We can infer from Alice's words that Williamson and his wife, Emma, were not well-off financially. Perhaps this was why he shifted his passion from his own research to guiding and teaching his students, and exploring how applied chemistry might be made relevant to industry and everyday life. Since he had mastered both practical and theoretical chemistry his teaching ranged widely, and his popularity among his students increased all the more.

In the autumn of 1856 Alex and Emma returned from their honeymoon trip to Germany, Switzerland and France, and settled into a large five-bedroom house at 16 Provost Road, Haverstock Hill. Their house was in a quiet residential area only a mile northwest of Alex's previous house in Hampstead, where he had spent his bachelor days. The elegant house stands there even today.

In order to fulfil the duties of his double professorship, Williamson worked extremely hard to prepare clearly argued lectures, which he saw as vital. There was a need for an assistant for this work, and he asked his former student Henry Roscoe to take up this post. In his letter to Roscoe he explained:

> my first act ... is to ask you to give the college the benefit of your services as assistant to the General Chemistry Class ... I intend giving the students exercises in the most important points taught in the lectures and shall be anxious to get the *whole class* to do them. These will of course have to be corrected, and in many cases it will be desirable to explain to individual students whatever they may have failed to understand in the lectures.[27]

Williamson's lectures were clear and impressive, and, for those eager to learn, his classes were very attractive. He sometimes took students on industrial tours. His method was not to begin by stating general principles, but rather to lead their minds towards these principles by comparing individual facts through demonstration and experiments. He used mechanical models when he wanted to explain chemical changes. In later years he used his own textbook *Chemistry for Students* (1865) in his teaching. The aim of the textbook is explained in the preface:

> This little book is intended to supply to students of chemistry an outline of the most interesting and useful facts pertaining to the science, and of the most important ideas that have been got from a study of those facts.[28]

Williamson standardised basic chemistry terminology to make it easier for beginners to understand easily, and his textbook went through many editions.

He often invited friends and research colleagues to his house in Provost Road. Among his guests were many students, as Williamson and his wife Emma always greatly enjoyed being surrounded by young people, and Emma was naturally gifted at entertaining. There were many who were attracted to her intelligent and kind personality. She gave Alex renewed courage to jump into yet more unknown worlds.

3
The Chōshū Five

Autumn 1863. A tea clipper docked at the Port of London. It was just after eight in the morning on 4 November. The name of the ship was the *Pegasus*. Among those who were busy loading and unloading were two Japanese, Bunta Shiji (aka Kaoru Inoue, 28 years old, Fig. 8) and Shunsuke Itō (aka Hirobumi Itō, 22 years old, Fig. 9). They had left Shanghai in late June, rounded the Cape of Good Hope, and reached their destination after four hard months of being treated as deck hands. It was their first voyage by sea and they were worn out both physically and mentally. Why did these two young men – who, together with Yōzō Yamao (Fig. 10), Yakichi Nomura (aka Masaru Inoue, Fig. 11) and Kinsuke Endō (Fig. 12), formed a group that has come to be generally known as the Chōshū Five – decide to leave Japan to come to London? The explanation lies in Japan's situation at that time.

Storm of capitalism hits Japan

It was the end of the Edo period, when Japan was under the rule of the Tokugawa shogunate, and the country was experiencing turbulence in both its politics and its economy. In 1853 Commodore Perry's 'black ships' – Western war vessels – arrived at Uraga near Edo (Tokyo) and following this incident Japan entered into friendship treaties with several Western countries. In 1858 trade treaties were signed with five of those countries as Japan abandoned its 200-year-old policy of national isolation, and took its first real steps towards opening its doors to foreign countries, and taking its place in the international community. While this was happening, Japan was mercilessly attacked by a storm of capitalist interests. Backed by their overwhelming military capability, Western powers such as Britain, the US, France and Russia

Fig. 8 Bunta (Kaoru) Inoue. Courtesy of JCII Camera Museum, Tokyo.

MAULL & Cọ

187ᴬ PICCADILLY
AND
62 CHEAPSIDE

Fig. 9 Shunsuke (Hirobumi) Itō. Courtesy of JCII Camera Museum, Tokyo.

Fig. 10   Yōzō Yamao. Courtesy of JCII Camera Museum, Tokyo.

Fig. 11 Yakichi Nomura (Masaru Inoue). Courtesy of JCII Camera Museum, Tokyo.

Fig. 12   Kinsuke Endō. Courtesy of Japan Mint Museum, Osaka.

were applying pressure on Japan to agree to free trade, just as they had done on China. Foreign settlements sprung up in port towns such as Yokohama and Nagasaki, as many foreign merchants arrived seeking commercial opportunities.

Under these circumstances some Japanese warriors tried to drive out and kill foreigners, blaming them for domestic political and economic turmoil, a movement known as *jōi*, or 'expel the barbarians'. The emperor in particular disliked foreigners, so the movement spread rapidly and gave rise to a new expression: *sonnō jōi*, 'revere the emperor and expel the barbarians'.

Behind these anti-foreign ideas lay a deep sense of crisis, as warriors feared Japan might be colonised by one of the Western powers. Many of those who shared this feeling were to be found in the powerful domains in western Japan, in Satsuma and Saga in Kyūshū, Chōshū in Chūgoku, and Tosa in Shikoku. They were to play leading roles during the Meiji Restoration, the political revolution that was followed by the resumption of practical imperial rule in 1868.

These western domains on the coast closest to Korea and China were well aware of the importance of coastal defence, and they had already been introducing Western naval military technology in areas such as shipbuilding, navigation, artillery, cannon casting and the construction of gun batteries. They had put great efforts into strengthening their military capabilities, so that as a result they now rivalled the power of the ruling house, the shogunate or *bakufu*.

From 1860, the *bakufu* had become seriously concerned at the number of incidents caused by increasingly fanatical warriors of the anti-foreign faction in various parts of the country. In July 1861 the British consulate based at Tōzen-ji in Edo was attacked by renegade warriors from the Mito domain and several diplomats suffered serious injuries. Then in September of the following year some British merchants on horseback were assaulted by Satsuma warriors in a village called Namamugi near Yokohama. One man was killed and two others were badly wounded. In January 1863 the British consulate under construction in Shinagawa, Edo, was attacked and burnt down by Chōshū warriors. Not surprisingly, these incidents scared the foreign community. Given this situation, the emperor ordered the *bakufu* to return to the old policy of national isolation and to expel all foreigners immediately. In response, the Shōgun Tokugawa Iemochi went to Kyoto for an audience with the emperor; it was the first time this had happened for 230 years. At the meeting it was decided that the policy of expelling foreigners would be put into practice in two months' time, on 25 June 1863. On hearing the decision, those warriors who supported the *sonnō jōi* faction, most of them from Chōshū, were enormously excited.

'Living machines'

Kaoru Inoue and Hirobumi Itō, from Chōshū, were both core supporters of the *sonnō jōi* movement. Together with Yōzō Yamao and Genzui Hisasaka, they had been thrilled to participate in the attack on the British consulate that was orchestrated by Shinsaku Takasugi, also from Chōshū. But a month later, in Kyoto, Kaoru Inoue met the military strategist Shōzan Sakuma and was greatly impressed by his arguments in favour of strengthening the navy, and the necessity of sending people abroad to study. He decided that he himself should go abroad and study Western naval science. Yamao reached the same conclusion; they both became convinced that this was a necessary first step to achieving true *jōi*.

They argued that strengthening Chōshū's military capability, and modernising and enriching their own domain, would lead to the modernisation of Japan as a whole; it would strengthen the coastal defences of Japan and avert the potential colonisation of the country. Senior members of the domain were impressed by their arguments and put forward their views to their lord, Takachika Mōri, and his heir, Sadahiro Mōri. On 4 June 1863, Kaoru Inoue and Yamao were notified that permission had been granted for them to go abroad to study, and a third member, Yakichi Nomura (aka Masaru Inoue, 20 years old), was added to the group. Kaoru Inoue was familiar with Western studies, and Yamao and Masaru Inoue had studied sailing and navigation. The lord's instructions to the three men read as follows:

> It is not easy to go abroad and study under the current circum-stances, but if we were to go into conflict with foreign powers it would be even more difficult to import their excellent technology. So I grant you five years of 'leave' and expect you to go to great lengths to achieve your aim. On your return I expect you to devote yourselves to the improvement and strengthening of our naval power.[29]

The three of them immediately set off for Yokohama, and started negotiating a means of passage and its cost with Samuel Gower, manager of Jardine Matheson's Yokohama office, whom they had previously met. It was not easy to persuade him but Samuel Gower finally agreed to help them. By then it was already late June.

At this stage, two more men joined them. They were Hirobumi Itō and Kinsuke Endō (27 years old), who were both eager to go abroad. Five brave young men; their destination Britain, their aim to study naval science.

By that time Jardine Matheson had become the largest of the foreign trading companies in Asia. They had opened their branch office in Yokohama as soon as the port was opened in 1859, and were on their way to becoming the leading trading company in Japan. The Japanese called their offices 'Lot Number One, Yokohama'. Ironically, it was this British trading company that was about to assist the illegal passage of Chōshū retainers who wished to 'expel the barbarians'. On 25 June, the day after Jardine Matheson agreed to help them, Chōshū implemented the policy of exclusion and attacked an American merchant vessel in the Straits of Shimonoseki. An analysis of the incident appeared in a Shanghai-based newspaper:

> The Pembroke is an American ship, and at the time of the attack was flying the American flag. The insult to which she was subjected

expresses plainly the determination of the Japanese government to expel all foreigners without regard to nationality, and announces the opening of a new era in Japanese history more dismal than any yet chronicled.[30]

Under the circumstances, going abroad was no easy matter and Kaoru Inoue and the four others were fully prepared to die if necessary. On 26 June, the day before they sailed, they wrote to the governing council of their domain:

> We are well aware of the gravity of our action. We took this decision knowing that our illegal act deserves the death sentence. If we fail to follow through with our original intention, we have not the slightest intention of coming back alive ... We humbly beg your understanding and forgiveness. Think of us merely as being 'living machines' that you have bought.

They made an impassioned plea for understanding, saying that it was a decision taken at the risk of losing their lives, and apologised for having borrowed a large amount of money. By using the expression 'living machines' they meant that they wished to be seen as men who would equip themselves with Western technology. For them it was a life-or-death journey in order to learn the technology necessary to withstand the barbarians; in other words, travelling abroad in order to expel the foreigners.

Opening their eyes to Western civilisation

That evening at around nine o'clock they arrived at 'Lot Number One, Yokohama', went through the ceremony of cutting their topknots, and changed into the Western clothes that Gower had prepared for them, a terrible humiliation. For them, going overseas at that time was tantamount to having to swallow their pride. On their departure, Itō showed his spirit by leaving a poem:

> As I leave
> Mindful of my shame as a man
> Know that I do so
> For my emperor and my land![31]

Past midnight, Gower let the five of them out of the back door and guided them to a small tender that took them to the *Chelswick*, a steamer that belonged to Jardine Matheson. Even on board they had to hide themselves in the coal bunker so as not to be discovered by officials. There they waited. Finally the ship steamed out of Yokohama before dawn on 27 June, just two days after Chōshū opened fire on a foreign vessel for the first time. They arrived in Shanghai five days later, and were astounded at the splendid sight of this booming modern centre of commerce. Seeing the naval might of foreign powers in Shanghai brought home to them Japan's vulnerability. It did not take them long to realise that *jōi* was a mistake that would ruin their country, and that it was essential for Japan to strengthen its naval defences. It must have been truly eye-opening for them to encounter representatives of Western civilisation at first hand in Shanghai.

Soon after arriving in the city and armed with a letter of introduction from Gower, they went to see William Keswick in Jardine Matheson's Shanghai office. Keswick asked them the reason of their trip. They meant to say 'to study the navy' but because of their poor English they replied 'navigation', so Keswick was left under the impression that they were going to Britain to learn to sail. He divided them into two groups, and put them on two sailing ships that were returning to London, asking the captains of the ships to give them some training during the voyage. Kaoru Inoue and Itō went on board the *Pegasus*, a small 300-ton ship, and the other three went on a slightly bigger boat, the *White Adder* (500 tons, Fig. 13). Both were tea clippers carrying tea from China to Britain.

The long journey from Shanghai was a hard challenge for Kaoru Inoue and Itō, and they were naturally overjoyed when the *Pegasus* arrived safely in London on 4 November. What they encountered was British civilisation at its height, and Inoue was struck dumb with shock. Reminiscing later, he said that he did not know what to do for a while. He wrote in his autobiography:

> Three- or five-storey buildings were lined up, trains were running in all directions, dark smoke from factories billowed high in the sky, and people came and went everywhere. These prosperous sights made me feel dazed when I first saw them and the idea of *jōi* completely disappeared from my mind in an instant.[32]

Steam locomotives threaded through high buildings made of brick or stone, black smoke was puffing out of the chimneys of modern

Fig. 13 The *White Adder*. Courtesy of Yamaguchi Prefectural Archive.

factories with modern facilities, and people were busily going about in the streets of the city. Seeing this in front of their eyes, both Kaoru Inoue and Itō clearly realised how unrealistic the idea of 'expelling the barbarians' was.

They were taken to Fenchurch Street station by train, then to a hotel in America Square on the eastern side of Minories. To their delight and surprise Masaru Inoue, Endō and Yamao had arrived before them and were waiting for them. Yamao was at a barber's shop at the time, which was quite a sight for them.

'A really good education'

A few days later, Captain Bowers of the *Pegasus* took them to Hugh Matheson, the managing director of Jardine Matheson. It appears that Bowers asked Matheson for his advice and assistance regarding the young Japanese men's life in Britain. Matheson recalled his encounter with the Japanese students as follows:

> On arrival in London, he [Captain Bowers] brought his young passengers to my office. Their names were Ito, Side (Kaoru Inoue),

Yamaou (Yōzō Yamao), Nomuran (Masaru Inoue), and Endo. Only Nomuran ventured at first to speak a little broken English. I undertook to get them suitably boarded, and to arrange for their education. I was extremely fortunate in inducing Dr Williamson, Professor of Chemistry in University College, afterwards President of the British Association, to receive them into his house. In conference with the professor, I arranged for them to learn some English, and be placed in classes where they would lay the groundwork of a really good education. In this respect Dr Williamson's advice was invaluable. To me they referred everything. 'How can we get our washing done?' 'Where can we buy a pair of shoes?' They made most diligent use of their time. I saw them frequently.[33]

It is worth noting Matheson's words: 'In this respect Dr Williamson's advice was invaluable'. Williamson must have explained to him how to go about laying the necessary groundwork for the Japanese students' proper education, based on his views on a comprehensive scientific education that he had been putting into practice in his own teaching at UCL. The fact that they were the first Japanese students who had come to study at UCL must have been a significant factor for Williamson. 'Unity out of difference' had been Williamson's lifelong aim, and seeing those Japanese students in front of him, he might well have seen this as a great opportunity to put his philosophy into practice.

Hugh Matheson had asked Sir Augustus Prevost, a councillor at UCL, to recommend someone who could be a mentor to the Japanese students. Williamson must have been an obvious choice for Prevost, who had much respect for Williamson's character, his ideals for education and above all his cosmopolitan outlook. In his obituary, Foster paid great tribute to the way Williamson went about his task with such sincerity:

In many respects, Williamson was admirably qualified to exercise a beneficial influence on the band of earnest young inquirers who were put under his care. He combined strength and decision of character with sound judgment and much kindliness of feeling, and his standard of personal conduct and honour was uniformly high, while his familiarity with the life of France and Germany, and with many of the leading men of those countries, gave him a wide outlook and a freedom from mere insular prejudices.[34]

Foster's words testify to Williamson's affectionate and magnanimous personality, which was free of prejudice.

The reception of the Japanese students

Williamson was 39 at that time and was in the prime of life (Fig. 14). A daughter, Alice, had been born to the Williamsons the year before in 1862, and he and Emma must have been busy bringing up their baby daughter. Alice would later marry Dr Alfred Henry Fison, a lecturer in physics at UCL, in 1888, and their descendants are still alive today.

H. J. WHITLOCK, PHOTO.   BIRMINGHAM

Fig. 14 Carte-de-visite photograph of Alexander Williamson by H.J. Whitlock, *c*. 1865. Science & Society Picture Library/Getty Images.

The year 1863 became a memorable one for Williamson, and not only because he took on responsibility for the Japanese students (Fig. 15). In 1862 he was awarded a Royal Medal by the Royal Society (Fig. 16), and in 1863 he was elected president of the Chemical Society of London, the highest post in the field of chemistry in Britain. Furthermore

MAULL & POLYBLANK   LONDON

Fig. 15   The Chōshū five. Courtesy of Hagi Museum.

Fig. 16 Royal Medal awarded to Williamson by the Royal Society. Courtesy of the Williamson collection/Phoebe Barr.

he was chosen to be the head of the Chemical Science section of the British Association at its general meeting held in Newcastle. But he was not the kind of person to indulge in the authority given to him. Foster quotes from an article in *Nature* (12 May 1904) in which Dr Thomas Edward Thorpe sketched Williamson's character:

> He has a high sense of duty, and of the responsibilities of his position as a representative man of science. Although, like many strong men, fond of power, he was in no sense a self-seeking man, and was contemptuous of the artifices by which smaller and more ambitious men seek to gain preferment.[35]

The five young men from Japan were lucky. They encountered a teacher rare in the world of education in Britain. Williamson invited them all to live in his commodious house in Provost Road. It could not have been easy for the couple with their newborn baby Alice and two servants, but they made these foreign visitors welcome. In the end, however, it proved impossible to house them all, so Matheson made an arrangement for Kaoru Inoue and Yamao to lodge with the Coopers at 103 Gower Street, in front of the College. Alexander Davis Cooper (1820–1888) was a fairly well-known painter specialising in genre painting. His father Abraham was a famous painter and a member of the Royal Academy, and his wife was also a painter who exhibited her works at the Academy.

Those who moved to the Coopers' must have lived in an artistic atmosphere surrounded by paintings. Williamson's house at 16 Provost Road and the Coopers' at 103 Gower Street are still there, and have changed little in appearance. Many Japanese students who came to London before and after the Meiji Restoration were to stay with the Coopers. Hisanari Murahashi from Satsuma lodged there in 1865, and Kosaburō Yamazaki and Teisuke Minami from Chōshū in 1866. After the Restoration, Tatsui Baba and Kenkichi Kataoka from Tosa stayed with the Coopers. One after the other, Japanese students came to this house on the recommendation of the first lodgers, Kaoru Inoue and Yamao. The place had become a gathering point for high-spirited warriors of the period around the Meiji Restoration. It must have been the Coopers' warm welcome towards those who arrived from a country in the Far East with high hopes that made the house so convivial and comfortable for their visitors.

But to digress for a moment: there is an interesting tale told about Mr Cooper, the artist.

On 15 December 1872, Takayoshi Kido (aka Kogorō Katsura) of Chōshū, one of the vice-ambassadors of the famous Iwakura Mission (see Chapter 6), visited Cooper's house with Chikanori Fukuhara and noted in his diary:

> Cloudy day. Around eleven, I visited an artist's house with Yoshiyama (Chikanori Fukuhara) and saw a portrait of our *daimyō* [feudal lord]. It was a good likeness and I have to admit that the artist must have been very skilled to have produced it without actually meeting the subject in question. I heard that Yamao once lodged in this house. Returned to Yoshiyama's after the visit.[36]

Kido, having seen Cooper's portrait of his *daimyo*, Takachika Mōri, was very impressed that the artist had managed to draw such a good likeness of someone without ever having met him. Cooper was known as a portrait painter. His drawing was probably based on illustrations of Mōri that appeared in articles relating to Japanese matters in the newspapers. In addition, what he heard from Kaoru Inoue and Yamao about their *daimyō* must have left a certain image in his mind. This painting might be hanging in a corner of someone's house, even today. An interesting thought. A little episode that illustrates an early link between Britain and Japan.

In search of the 'essence of the West'

The time came for the five Japanese to start their studies at UCL. They were accepted with the status of 'students not matriculated' in the Faculty of Arts and Laws to which Williamson belonged. They chose their subjects, paid their fees and attended lectures. We can trace their choice of subjects on the Register of Students kept in UCL's archives (Fig. 17).

In 1863, Itō, Yamao, Masaru Inoue and Endō all took the analytical chemistry course. It must have been an obvious choice, as Williamson was in charge of it. Kaoru Inoue's name is missing, perhaps because he failed to pay by the deadline. Kaoru Inoue and Itō returned to Japan before the beginning of the 1864 academic year. The rest of the students continued studying analytical chemistry; Yamao added chemistry and civil engineering, Masaru Inoue took chemistry, geology and mineralogy; and Endō's choices were chemistry, geology and mineralogy for both 1864 and 1865. For 1866 only Masaru Inoue remained in UCL, as Yamao moved to Glasgow, and Endō returned home. In his third year, Masaru Inoue took English, French, mathematics and mathematical physics in addition to his initial choice of analytical chemistry, geology and mineralogy. His choice of subjects indicates clearly that he was faithfully following Williamson's idea of a liberal arts education. In his third year he was completing the 'foundation building' that is essential for higher education.

Williamson's Birkbeck Laboratory was the centre of the Japanese students' university life. As already mentioned, the aim of the training was to develop technology and applied skills through work in analytical chemistry in the laboratory, while learning basic science subjects in a systematic way. Williamson's aim was to teach the essence of scientific research by learning chemistry from both sides, theoretical and practical.

In later years Itō reminisced as follows:

> During the day we were at university, and we also studied at home early in the morning and during the evenings. We lodged with a chemistry professor Williamson, who taught us mathematics. To put it more clearly, the teacher was at university during the day and taught chemistry, and he gave us lessons in the early morning and evening at home. We studied at the university during the day. That's the kind of thing we did.[37]

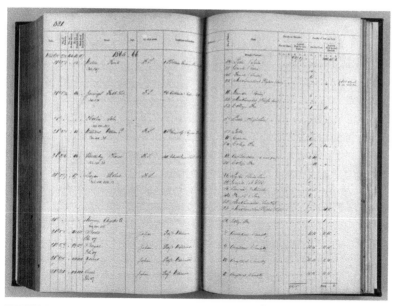

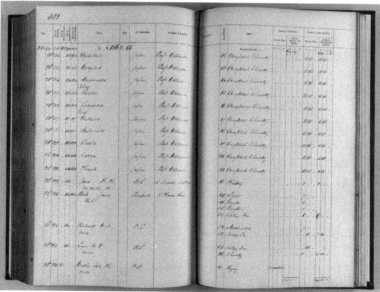

Fig. 17 Pages from UCL's student register, 1863–6. Courtesy of UCL Special Collections.

Gradually they settled into the liberal academic atmosphere at UCL. They experienced radical education with a practical approach and absorbed its underlying principles.

Between classes they visited the Royal Mint and many museums and art galleries, as well as shipbuilding yards and factories. They were eager to observe Western civilisation in action. They had pledged to become 'living machines' with Western knowledge. To achieve this aim, it was not enough simply to accumulate knowledge through academic work and to master a few technologies; they also needed to discover the 'essence of the West'. But this was elusive.

Emma played a significant role in their understanding. J. Harris and W.H. Brock commented in their paper on Williamson:

> They had, in addition, the advantage of coming under the kindly influence of Mrs Williamson, who not only made them feel members of the family and did everything in her power to make their stay in England a happy one, but also assisted in their tuition in learning English. The students made amazingly rapid progress with the English language, and quickly acquired a sound knowledge of British industry and commerce, a knowledge which they were soon to apply with such success to the development of their own country.[38]

Emma was careful to ensure that they became familiar with Western civilisation in their everyday life.

Alexander Williamson, meanwhile, not only sent them to see many industrial plants, but also took them himself. Having shown them several experiments in his laboratory, he took them to factories so that they could see such experiments applied in practice. He wanted them first of all to understand the scientific principles, and then to think for themselves about the real nature of modern science-based culture. His philosophy of 'unity out of difference' and his belief that 'civilisation blossoms only by harmonising diverse cultures of individuals and states'[39] led him to this path, and the five Japanese students responded remarkably well to his teaching.

On 22 January 1864 they visited the Bank of England on Threadneedle Street, probably at Williamson's suggestion. The Bank had the best technology for producing bank notes in Europe at that time, and impressed visitors by its high technological standards, printing several thousand notes at a time. The record of the Japanese students' visit can still be seen today. On a £1,000 note, printed to mark their visit, they signed their names in both roman letters and *kanji* (Fig. 18). This was only

Fig. 18 £1,000 note, printed to mark the visit of the Chōshū five, 1864. © Bank of England.

done for special guests. In the border at the bottom, their visit is recorded as 'A Daimio – and three Native friends – Japanese 22nd Jany. 1864'.

The term *daimyō* was already known in Europe as the word meaning a feudal lord, and it appeared in diplomatic documents, so the five students from Chōshū may well have used the word to give themselves some authority. Kaoru Inoue, as the oldest and the 'leader' of the group, signed his name as 'Sidi Bunta' in large letters on the left-hand side. It seems likely that he called himself a *daimyō*, and also wrote the other names for his companions as well. The Bank's note saying 'three Native friends' seems to be a simple error for 'four Native friends'.

They must have been truly amazed by the level of technology displayed in the Bank of England, which was a most advanced example of the era, and they began to grasp what the civilisation brought into being by Western sciences really meant.

For a new Japan

Not long after the five had visited the Bank of England, Hugh Matheson paid them a visit with the grave news from Japan that there had been a military conflict between Britain and Satsuma in August of the previous year. He was referring to the Anglo-Satsuma War (1863). They had probably heard a little about this event already from the British press, which reported on a series of incidents and Chōshū's attack on foreign vessels, followed by foreign retaliation, and the war in Satsuma.

Looking back on those days, Kaoru Inoue wrote:

Articles arguing the need for reprisals against Chōshū began to appear in the newspapers, which made us feel very depressed. I talked over the situation with Itō. Even if we did manage to attain naval expertise, such knowledge would be useless if our country ceased to exist, I argued. We were wasting our time. The two of us should go back, meet our *daimyō* and other officials, explain the situation in Europe, and persuade them to change tack, and adopt the 'revere the emperor and open up the country' policy. Itō completely agreed with me so we decided that we should return home immediately, leaving the other three in Britain.[40]

Kaoru Inoue could clearly see how advanced Western culture and technology was, and he was acutely aware of how far behind Japan was in those respects. The sense of crisis that he felt led him to advocate opening up the country, together with the slogans 'a strong military' and 'a prosperous country'.

Itō, reminiscing about his time in Britain, said: 'in Europe I observed that countries prospered with a prefectural system, and I became convinced that our own feudal system had to be abolished'.[41] In their minds they were already considering Japan as a unified nation, and were developing their own ideas on how to unite a divided country.

A letter, signed by all five students, was sent to Matheson telling him that after much consideration they had decided to send Kaoru Inoue (Fig. 19) and Itō back to Japan so that they could save Japan from defeat by foreign countries. Those around the Chōshū students tried to change their minds, saying it was too dangerous to go back, but they were determined.

Masaru Inoue, Endō and Yamao were also willing to go back to Japan, but Kaoru Inoue pointed out the importance of following through with their original intention of serving the country by becoming 'living machines', and he managed to persuade them to stay on. It was towards the end of April 1864 that Kaoru Inoue and Itō left London for Japan.

Fig. 19 Yakichi Nomura (Masaru Inoue). Courtesy of the Williamson collection/Phoebe Barr.

At the end of June, two months after their departure, the remaining three, Masaru Inoue, Endō and Yamao, met Reginald Russell, a British diplomat. He had visited Japan in June 1861 as attaché to the first secretary of the British legation in Japan, Laurence Oliphant, and had stayed on for two years to learn Japanese. It is probable that Russell, who knew that the combined forces of Britain, America, France and the Netherlands were planning to attack the batteries at Shimonoseki, approached these Japanese students in order to find out the real situation in Chōshū. Lord John Russell, the foreign secretary, was not in favour of the plan for a military expedition to Shimonoseki that had been drawn up by Sir Rutherford Alcock, the British envoy to Japan.

According to Reginald Russell, the students told him:

> that their master [i.e. the Chōshū *daimyō* Môri] had hoped, by the desperate expedient of aggression of [sic: against] Europeans, to obtain this object; to cause the overthrow of the Tycoon's 'dishonest government', which 'had become hateful to all right-thinking Japanese', and to restore peace and order in the country, not by the expulsion of foreigners (as, said they, the Taikun's Govt. falsely represented to us was the object and desire of all its own opponents) but by restoring to the Mikado, their rightful Emperor, the power which the Taikuns had usurped from him for so many years. Their prince, they said, and many other powerful Daimios, as well as, in fact, the great mass of the nation, hoped that by embroiling the Tycoon with the great 'Powers of the West', they would in the first place weaken him, and enable the Japanese people to restore the power to their rightful sovereign, and secondly, 'that the veil would at length fall from the eyes of foreigners, and that they would see that no treaty they could make with the Taikun would be binding, or beneficial in any way, because it was not sanctioned or recognised by the true Emperor', nor, consequently, by the national feeling throughout the country; and that then the foreign powers would make a Treaty directly with their Emperor, the Mikado, which should be recognized and respected by all people in their country, which would thus extend to all classes and parties the benefits of foreign intercourse and trade. At present, they said, the 'dishonest government' of the Tycoon usurped to itself all these advantages … They said … that if he [the emperor] knew more about foreigners, that is, if they were to address themselves to him at Kioto that he would be easily induced to make a Treaty with them himself, which, said Nagato's men [i.e. the men from Chōshū], all Japanese must then respect. … 'And', they said, 'the advantages of a treaty made with the Mikado would be equally great for foreigners and Japanese; for you could then live in security for your lives and property in our country; and we should no longer have any civil war amongst ourselves; whilst Japanese of all classes would share equally the benefits of intercourse and commerce with you, the profits of which now go only into the pockets of the Tycoon's officers.'[42]

Reginald Russell and the Japanese students had two meetings and they spoke both in English and in Japanese. What Russell gathered from these meetings was that they had come to Britain to study 'applied sciences' and 'such arts as might be useful to their countrymen' and to learn European languages. They further explained why two of their number had returned 'to report back everything that they had experienced and request that more students should be sent to Europe'.[43] They disguised the true reason that Kaoru Inoue and Itō had gone back to Japan. Perhaps they did believe that Japan might indeed be saved if more of the *jōi* faction experienced European civilisation. They hoped that the court, rather than the *bakufu*, would be persuaded to sign treaties with the foreign powers and so restore peace and order. In their reply to Russell they emphasised the 'applied sciences' and useful 'technology' rather than 'naval expertise', and that six months into the studies at UCL they had gained a clearer sense of what they wanted to do: 'become men who would be of use in the modernisation of Japan'. Their excellent results at UCL showed the depth of their dedication. At the end of the 1864 academic year, Yamao came fourth and Endō fifth in the applied chemistry course, and they were both awarded diplomas with distinction. In the hearts of these five students, including the two who had returned home, there was a clear vision of a unified Japan.

4
The Satsuma Nineteen

On 9 February 1864 the House of Commons was in uproar, as a heated debate erupted over the rights and wrongs of the Anglo-Satsuma War of August 1863. Several MPs were critical, arguing that the bombardment by the British fleet, burning down the town of Kagoshima and causing casualties among innocent civilians, was inhumane behaviour unworthy of a civilised country. Many of those who shared these criticisms were members of Gladstone's Liberal Party, which was promoting anti-imperialism and free trade from the 'Little Englandism' point of view. Their reaction could be seen as expressing their rivalry with the Conservative Party led by Benjamin Disraeli. It was rare that an issue concerning a small country like Japan occasioned such a heated discussion in the House. The outcome was that Parliament adopted a motion that the British government should issue a statement of regret to the Japanese government. On the following day, *The Times* reported the event in detail under the heading 'Burning of Kagoshima'.

While this debate was going on in London, a peace agreement between Satsuma and Britain had already been reached in Japan.

Lessons from the Anglo-Satsuma War

The background to the war was as follows. In August 1862, four Britons were attacked in the post-station of Namamugi in Kanagawa by guards of the Satsuma domain (the so-called Namamugi Incident). Britain interpreted this incident as an act of *jōi*, and demanded substantial reparations from both the *bakufu* and Satsuma, as well as the immediate arrest and execution of the perpetrators. The *bakufu* reluctantly accepted this demand and paid up simply to avoid any further conflict, but Satsuma refused. Britain then adopted strong-arm tactics, dispatching seven ships to Kagoshima, the capital of Satsuma. On 15 August 1863, negotiations broke down and the British immediately set about bombarding Kagoshima. The result was that all the Satsuma gun emplacements were completely destroyed and the central part of Kagoshima was burnt down. Even on the British side there were many casualties, and both sides learned much from the conflict.

This short conflict had significant influence on Satsuma. As a result of this somewhat reckless battle, Satsuma came to realise the power of European civilisation and the absurdity of trying to simply expel foreigners. The result was a reversal of policy in favour of going it alone, relying on increasing the wealth and military power of the domain itself rather than the country as a whole. In other words, the Satsuma domain took steps to open itself up to outside influence, a move of great historical significance.

Soon after the conflict ended, an appetite for rapprochement grew on both sides and through the mediation of Tadahiro Shimazu, *daimyō* of the Sadohara domain, direct talks between Britain and Satsuma began on 9 November in Yokohama. The talks were successfully concluded on 11 December. Satsuma not only agreed to pay reparations, but also expressed a wish to buy warships from Britain and to send some students to study in Britain.

It must have been a surprise for Britain to hear so soon from Satsuma, with whom it had so recently been in conflict, that they wanted to buy warships and send their students to learn from their opponents. Britain quickly realised that Satsuma was not of the *jōi* faction, as it had assumed, but was actually among those elements in Japan who had been advocating the opening up of their doors to trade with foreign countries. The *New York Times*, on 30 January 1864, reported the events as follows:

> During the negotiations of Satsuma's Ambassadors with the English Ministers, they proposed to send to Europe thirty of their young men, to be educated in the useful arts, especially shipbuilding, cannon-making, &c. They expressed also a wish to buy a man-of-war, fully armed and equipped. This they were told they could do from any of the Western nations, provided peace was established, but intimated to them that, with the present state of things, it could not be done.

On 11 December 1863 Satsuma paid Britain the reparations as promised, the sum of £2,500, and Britain issued a note guaranteeing assistance in purchasing warships. Relations quickly improved, and Britain began to entertain the idea of a new central government, replacing the *bakufu* with a consortium of powerful domains with Satsuma at its core.

After the war, great efforts were made by Satsuma to expand its military power, particularly its navy, and to modernise the country following Western models. It was obvious that in order for this to succeed a strong financial base was key. There then appeared on the scene a man called Tomoatsu Godai (Fig. 20), with ideas of how to

Fig. 20 Tomoatsu Godai. Courtesy of JCII Camera Museum, Tokyo.

strengthen the economy. At the time of the conflict with Britain, which together with Kōan Matsuki (aka Munenori Terashima, Fig. 21) he had opposed, he had given himself voluntarily to the British and had been taken prisoner.

Fig. 21 Hiroyasu Matsuki (Munenori Terashima). Courtesy of JCII Camera Museum, Tokyo.

After being released in Yokohama, he travelled around the country and in June 1864, while in hiding in Nagasaki,[44] he was allowed to return to Satsuma. There he immediately presented a formal proposal in which he exposed the true nature of nineteenth-century international affairs, where the strong devoured the weak. Enriching the country and strengthening its military power by opening up to the world was, he argued, the way things had to be in this world. Citing the case of India and China, he rejected the idea of 'revere the emperor and expel the barbarians' as utterly foolish. The defeat in the recent conflict, he said, was an invaluable experience, because it made the people of Japan recognise the need to catch up with the level of industrial and military progress that the West had made in recent decades. He argued that Satsuma should take this opportunity and push hard to enrich the domain and strengthen the military ahead of other domains, because 'the early bird gets the worm'. He had two suggestions: start trading with Shanghai, and send students to Europe.

As we have seen, the latter had already been proposed by Satsuma at the time of the peace negotiations, so one can assume that the domain began preparations to send young men to Britain without delay. In November, Kakutarō Ishikawa, a lecturer at the domain academy, the Kaiseijo, sent Toshimichi Ōkubo a proposal for sending students abroad. The senior members of the clan deliberated and agreed to select several students from the academy and send them abroad to study naval and military science, just as Godai had proposed. The academy was an educational institution that had been established in July 1864 to encourage study of the West. In addition to military science, students learned astronomy, geography, navigation, shipbuilding and physics. Satsuma chose Britain with the hope of strengthening friendly ties with the country, and the selected students were expected to study the political systems, military power, geography and customs of Western countries.

The Satsuma students set sail

The selection of students started in December, and by February 1865 15 students and four supervising officers had been chosen (see p. 115; Figs 22, 23).

Most were in their early twenties. Some were supporters of *jōi* but it was hoped that they would see the error of their ways once they had been exposed to Western culture and technology. Hisanari Machida, as

Fig. 22 The Satsuma students. Courtesy of Kagoshima Prefectural Library.

Fig. 23 The Satsuma students. Courtesy of Kagoshima Prefectural Library.

an 'envoy', was to be in charge of the students, and Munenori Terashima and Tomoatsu Godai were assigned to study diplomacy, and industry and trade, respectively, and to negotiate and arrange the students' study visits.

As Satsuma had requested at the third peace conference after the Anglo-Satsuma War, eight students were to study naval science and three to study military science; two were to study medicine and one English. One must assume that by this time the British government had been informed through unofficial channels of Satsuma's plan to send such a mission, designed to strengthen relationships between Britain and the domain. In fact, the mission did not have the *bakufu*'s permission and was therefore illegal, and everyone on the mission must have been aware of this. They all travelled under assumed names and some kept their new names when they later returned to Japan. Under these circumstances, they decided to avoid a conspicuous departure from Nagasaki and instead set sail from the small port of Hashimaura, in the district of Kushikinogō in the northern part of the domain. The party, nineteen of them in total, left early in the morning of 17 April 1865 on board the *Australian*, a small steamship which had been arranged by Thomas Blake Glover, a Scottish merchant in Nagasaki. They were transferred to a large steamboat at Hong Kong and from there enjoyed a luxurious voyage. Two months later they arrived at their destination, Southampton, at dawn on 21 June. Late in the afternoon they went by train to London, where they arrived just after eight in the evening.

Given that it was eight o'clock in midsummer, London was not dark yet and they were astounded at what they saw: tall, magnificent, massive buildings the like of which they had never seen before. They felt as if they were in a dream. The South Kensington Hotel, where they stayed, was at 19 Queen's Gate Terrace, to the south of Kensington Park. Now used as offices, it seems that it was a reasonably good hotel at the time. Junzō Matsumura noted on 21 June: 'The hotel is beautiful. My room is No. 72 on the seventh floor and I finally managed to find it by following the room numbers. The accommodation is one pound a day.'[45] It was their first experience of staying in a Western-style hotel.

Starting their studies

During their stay in London, the students were looked after by Ryle Holme, an employee of Glover & Co. who had accompanied the mission all the way from Satsuma, and Glover's elder brother James Lindley

Glover. Glover & Co. was the acting agent of Jardine Matheson in Nagasaki, so it is likely that Holme and Glover went to see Hugh Matheson in London to ask his advice on how to arrange for the Japanese students to begin their studies. Hugh Matheson had been in a similar situation a year and half earlier while looking after the five students from Chōshū, so he must have mentioned Williamson.

Hatakeyama's diary on 22 June, the day after their arrival in London, records the following:

> Both James and Holme came to see us early in the morning and told us that they had been consulting with various people regarding our 'training'. As for our studies, according to the British system there are two months vacation per year and for the moment there are no lectures. So since our English is not good enough at the moment, the proposal is that we take advantage of this break to improve our conversational skills. It was decided that the best way would be to employ a teacher who would live with us and improve our English for the next two to three months.[46]

Everybody agreed. They moved to a flat in Bayswater Road, about a mile and half north of the hotel, and by the afternoon of 22 June they had settled in. Two days later, while they were practising conversation and reading by themselves, Holme and James arrived with a man called Barff, who, after some persuasion, had agreed to live in as their teacher. Frederick Settle Barff (1822–1886) was a former student of Williamson. After graduating from Cambridge he had become a deacon in the Catholic church. He had a talent for making stained glass and painting frescos. In 1864 he started studying chemistry under Williamson at UCL and was later chosen to be Williamson's assistant. For a short period he also worked as an assistant lecturer of chemistry and published, among other works, *An Introduction to Scientific Chemistry* (1869), which was reprinted many times. He went on to hold other positions including the professorship of chemistry at the short-lived Catholic University College, Kensington. At the time Barff joined the Japanese students to teach English he was working for Williamson, who must have recommended him to Holme and Glover.

There is a photograph of Barff in Arinori Mori's album; it shows him with a splendid beard and a direct, clergyman-like expression. Barff moved in with the Satsuma students on 25 June, and that evening Holme and James arrived with very surprising information. Hatakeyama recorded that:

Holme says that he came across some men from Chōshū on his way back the day before, and he saw them again today. I have no detailed information at the moment but three of them apparently came here the year before and have been studying 'chemistry'.[47]

The three Chōshū men were obviously Yōzō Yamao, Masaru Inoue and Kinsuke Endō. Holme and James must have heard from Matheson about these men, and Williamson had probably mentioned them too, but this was the first time that they had met them. Large as London was, in fact they were bound to meet them on the street at some stage or other. This was the first time the Satsuma students had heard of the young men from Chōshū and it must have come as a tremendous shock to discover that there were others who had illegally left Japan.

Satsuma meets Chōshū

On 2 July, a week after their encounter with Holme and James, the three students from Chōshū came to see the Satsuma students at their flat. Arriving at around six in the evening, they explained how they had come to Britain and how their studies were progressing; it was well after 11 when they left. The Satsuma students were initially somewhat taken aback, but gradually, as they talked, the feeling of being Japanese helped them overcome the difficulty of coming from rival domains.

The Satsuma students were given thorough preparatory training in both English and chemistry, undoubtedly helped by Williamson's experience of having dealt with the students from Chōshū. On 26 June, Barff went to the College and came back with blank notebooks, asking the students to write down what they learned. On 28 June, Hisanari Machida noted in his diary: 'We had no books up to that point but that evening some books of mathematics and other exercise books arrived.'[48]

Machida went to UCL on 4 July together with Barff and Munenori Terashima, and met up with the students from Chōshū, to see where they would be studying.

On 7 July two additional teachers called Graham and Valery arrived to teach them English. Charles Graham was Williamson's assistant at that time. He had first studied at Kennington Agricultural College, where John Nesbit was Professor of Chemistry, and in 1863 he had come to UCL, where he studied analytical chemistry under Williamson for two years. After being granted the degree of Bachelor of Science with an excellent academic record, he was immediately given the position of Williamson's assistant. He was awarded a doctorate in 1866. Between

1873 and 1878 he was a lecturer in the Chemistry Department and when a new Chair of Chemical Technology was established in 1878 he was elected as the first holder and remained in post until 1889.

While the Satsuma students were studying English and basic chemistry with Barff and Graham, they would often go sightseeing in the company of Yamao. On 25 July, for example, they met up at the Birkbeck Laboratory and visited the Tower of London, particularly its exhibition room of arms, and various shipbuilding yards. Hatakeyama noted in his diary that their gathering point was 'the chemistry place'. It must have been an extraordinary experience for them to see the machines and latest equipment in the Birkbeck Laboratory, which would soon become the focal point of their studies at UCL. Williamson, his assistants and students gathered there day and night to discuss and conduct experiments. It was the centre of their research. It was here that the Satsuma students were trained, and where they began to grasp what modern science really was. Without Williamson's considerable effort and help, this could not have been possible. A testimony to how hard Williamson worked on behalf of those Japanese students can be seen in his letter to Charles Atkinson, Secretary of the Council, dated 24 July:

> I should be glad to obtain the permission of the Council for a course of laboratory instruction of a somewhat exceptional kind which is now needed by a party of 14 Japanese Students. These young men cannot avail themselves of the full laboratory course but wish to enter the laboratory as students for one year, working only 3 or 4 hours per day. I propose that a fee of fifteen guineas be charged for the 12 months course.
>
> No special arrangements will need to be made by the College for the purpose of their instruction as *my assistants will do all that is needed*. The arrangement will not keep other students out of the laboratory by half-filling it as these young Japanese can work in the laboratory contiguous to the lecture room.[49]

Williamson had started making arrangements for the Satsuma students so that they could start their studies at UCL in the autumn (Fig. 24).

Britannia Iron Works

As a part of their preliminary field trips, Williamson took the students to the Britannia Iron Works in Bedford. The factory was well known for manufacturing state-of-the-art agricultural machinery. Niiro, Godai and

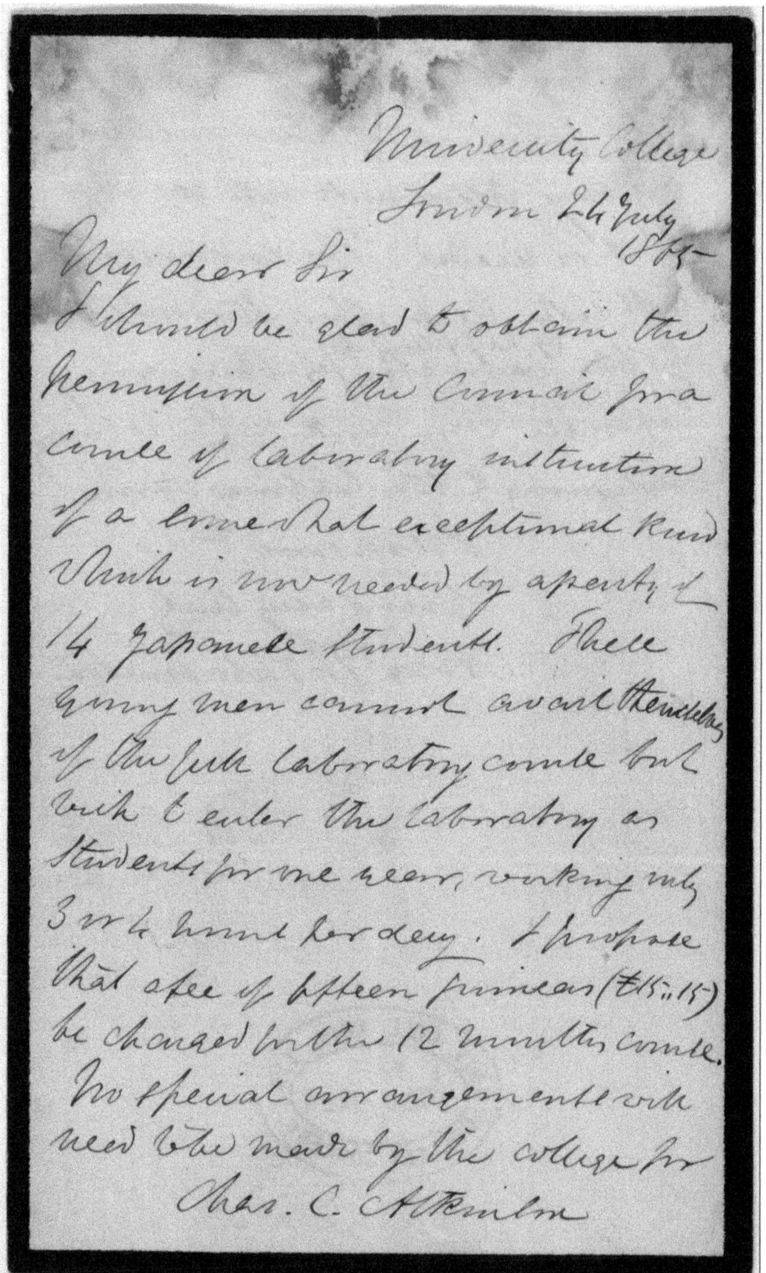

Fig. 24 Williamson's letter to Charles Atkinson, 24 July 1865. Courtesy of UCL Special Collections.

Hori, in their role as observers, six or seven Satsuma students including Machida, Hatakeyama and Nagoya, and two Chōshū students, Yamao and Masaru Inoue, as well as Graham and Foster, joined Williamson for the visit.

They received a citywide welcome, including from the mayor himself. The *Bedfordshire Times*, on 2 August 1865, reported their visit as follows:

On Saturday last a large party of Japanese, sent over by the Princes of that country to gain a knowledge of the agriculture and manufactures of Great Britain, paid a visit to the Britannia Iron Works. They were accompanied by Professor Williamson of the London University, by the Professor of Natural Philosophy at the Glasgow University, and other eminent scientific men, who have the direction of their investigations. The Japanese, whose remarkable physique caused considerable interest, the Mongolian type being very striking, took great interest in the machinery and various processes in operation at these important works, and seemed astonishingly quick in comprehending the various details. They appeared very unwilling to leave the works, but steam having been got up in one of the new steam-ploughing engines, about 15 of the Japanese crowded on to it wherever they could get a footing; and it was highly amusing to see with what delight they travelled in all directions over the extensive quadrangle of the works. After spending about three hours here they took luncheon with our worthy Mayor (Mr Jas Howard), and proceeded to witness the steam ploughing on Messrs Howard's farm at Clapham, where their amazement seemed to culminate, the operations being so much more simple than they had anticipated. A reaping machine which was at work was quickly handled and cleverly managed by them. Subsequently they visited Biddenham for the purpose of viewing Mr Charles Howard's celebrated shorthorns and sheep; and after dining with the Mayor they left for London by the last train, expressing their unbounded delight with the day's visit to Bedford, and their admiration of our English hospitality.

The journalist of the *Bedfordshire Times* seems to have been impressed by the Japanese students' response, and how quickly they grasped things they had not seen before. Williamson's practical teaching outside the classroom was having its effect even before they entered university.

Lodging at the homes of academics

At the beginning of August, as the university term was approaching, Williamson recommended that the Satsuma students lodge, two by two, at the homes of UCL academics. His idea made sense both educationally and financially. Arinori Mori stayed with Charles Graham, and there remains a photograph of Graham in Mori's album. It was a *carte de visite*, produced in a photographic studio in Berwick-upon-Tweed, close to the Scottish border, where Graham was born. It shows a fine, intelligent face. Mori had deep respect for him and wrote on the back of the photograph, 'teacher of science, I call him "father" as I'm staying with his family'.

Niiro, to show thanks for Williamson's kind consideration and assistance, had a contract drawn up on 4 August to pay him a fee of £400 per year. He reported back home, writing to Ōkubo and the others:

> Professor Williamson of London University is a famous person in Europe. He is much respected and trusted. Through Holme I have requested him to give assistance to our students. He has taken on the task most willingly and has been a father figure for our students. He very kindly made arrangements for our students' lodgings from the beginning of the month, and they are now staying with families two or three together. They have started attending classes and making progress. Unlike those from Chōshū who have been here for two years, our students are all 'properly brought up and trained' and are all well thought of. It has been decided that we pay a fee of £400 per year to Williamson. You may find this expensive but we cannot go against the custom of this country.[50]

It is interesting to find such a spirit of rivalry between Satsuma and Chōshū in the letter. Niiro was discovering that university teachers were in prestigious positions with much authority, and seems to have been much impressed that someone in such an important position was willing to take care of the students from Satsuma.

The students' activities

When most students moved into their allocated lodgings in London, Hikosuke Isonaga (Fig. 25) – at 13, the youngest student – left for Aberdeen with Thomas Glover's brother James on 19 August. He was too

Fig. 25 Hikosuke Isonaga (Kanae Nagasawa). Courtesy of Satsuma Students Museum, Kagoshima.

young to go to university and had promised Glover before leaving Japan that he would stay with Glover's family in Scotland and attend the local school. Yamao from Chōshū was also planning to go to Scotland around the same time. He had been much influenced by Williamson's emphasis on practical science and was anxious to put what he had learned into practice, but he lacked the funds. The Chōshū students were in serious financial difficulty as funds were no longer being sent from their domain. One day Yamao came to see the Satsuma student Machida. He told him that he wanted to go to Glasgow and work in a dockyard there but could not afford the train fare, and he asked if he could possibly borrow some money. Having given much thought to this request, Machida decided to ask his fellow students from Satsuma to help. Official funds could not be used for this, so each Satsuma student donated £1 and altogether they lent Yamao £16. This episode shows us how these students, casting aside the fact that they came from different domains, were beginning to work together as fellow countrymen.

Yamao managed to get to Glasgow that autumn. He worked at Napier Shipyard during the day, and continued his studies at Anderson's University in the evening. He never forgot the kindness of the Satsuma students and often wrote to them reporting how he was getting on. He was concerned about the welfare of the young Kanae Nagasawa (Hikosuke Isonaga) in Aberdeen, and kept in touch with him. Yamao wrote that, according to the Glovers, Kanae Nagasawa was very well and he had become just like a local boy, and had been achieving high marks and was awarded a distinction. At the bottom of his letter he added his new address, 177 West Regent Street, Glasgow. Regardless of the distance and time, the companionship and friendship of the Satsuma and Chōshū students was never disrupted.

In the meantime, Endō began to feel weak and show some symptoms of tuberculosis, so Matheson persuaded him to return to Japan. He left London for home at the beginning of the following year, 1866. Matheson's memoir records:

> About a year later [after the departure of Inoue and Ito], Endo who had shown signs of pulmonary complaint, was advised to return home. The two who remained, Yamaou (Yōzō Yamao) and Nomuran (Masaru Inoue), made great progress. I sent them to Glasgow, Newcastle, and other places to study mining, ship-building, and other large industries. Nomuran (Masaru Inoue) joined a regiment of Rifle Volunteers. They remained five years, and then returned to Japan with an excellent training.[51]

Alongside Williamson's education on the practical side, Matheson seems to have given the Japanese students significant assistance in all areas. Why did Yamao not ask him for some financial assistance when he wanted to go to Glasgow and instead asked the Satsuma students to help? Perhaps he was too proud to borrow money from the British.

On 21 October 1865, the 14 young men from Satsuma registered themselves at UCL as 'unmatriculated students', still using their assumed names. As arranged, they paid 15 guineas each to attend Williamson's analytical chemistry course. There is also a record that three days earlier, on 18 October, Nomura (Masaru Inoue) from Chōshū paid £7 to take mathematical physics.

As the term started, the students from Chōshū and Satsuma began to act like a group. In the positive scientific environment of UCL, they learned a great deal, and they gradually developed a cosmopolitan sense, stimulated by the international academic atmosphere. In their circle were not only Williamson, but also those Victorian intellectuals with whom they were lodging. Along with the people from UCL who were giving them academic guidance, there were also entrepreneurs such as Hugh Matheson, James Glover, the MP Laurence Oliphant and artists such as the painter Cooper.

On 7 March 1866, George Price Boyce (1826–1897), a well-known watercolourist, invited Hatakeyama and Yoshida to his house. *Japonisme* was at its peak in the London art world. The painter Dante Gabriel Rossetti (1828–1882), who founded the Pre-Raphaelites, was the central figure on the art scene of the time, and he and his friends were eager to learn about the real Japan. Hearing that some Japanese young men were living in London, Boyce immediately invited two of them to his house and introduced them to his '*japonisant*' group.

Hatakeyama and Yoshida must have met the artists George Dunlop Leslie (1835–1921) and Rossetti, as well as Boyce. They told them about traditional art and life in Japan, and explained why they had come all the way to England. Rossetti and his fellow artists must have felt that they found 'true Japan' in these young men. No doubt they saw in them an aesthetic sensibility that valued innocent, pure and well-balanced beauty, characteristic of Japanese fine arts and crafts such as *ukiyo-e*, or pictures of the floating world, and pottery. For those Victorian avant-garde artists, who were tired of their own artificial, vulgar, mechanised culture, the young Japanese students were probably a breath of fresh air. So these young men played a part in introducing Japanese culture to the West.

The arrival of a new family member

Towards the end of 1865, the Williamsons moved to a bigger house at 12 Fellows Road, less than half a mile east of their house in Provost Road. Masaru Inoue continued to live with the family, and he used to help out in the house. The Satsuma students were invited every month or so, and Masaru Inoue acted as a waiter. Emma was pregnant at the time, and gave birth to a boy, Oliver Key Williamson (Fig. 26), in March of the following year. As an adult he would fulfil the hopes of his parents by becoming a respected physician specialising in paediatrics. He married Edith Gertrude Edington in December 1911 at the age of 45, and the couple lived in Farnham, Surrey. In 1922 Oliver went to Johannesburg to work in a hospital, and returned to England in retirement.

Fig. 26 Oliver Key Williamson as child. Courtesy of the Williamson collection/Phoebe Barr.

5
The fate of the early students

Around the time that the Satsuma students started taking Williamson's analytical chemistry course at UCL in autumn 1865, two more young men from Chōshū arrived in London. The first was Teisuke Minami (18 years old), a cousin of Shinsaku Takasugi, the leader of Chōshū's reforming group; the second was Kosaburō Yamazaki (21 years old), a navy officer. Takasugi had persuaded Minami to go abroad even though it was still illegal. Minami left Shimonoseki together with Yamazaki with the help of Thomas Glover, and they arrived in London in November, after 130 days on a sailing ship via Shanghai. They were so badly off that they could hardly afford to buy food and basic clothes, and they were lucky to be able to move temporarily into a room at the Coopers' after Yamao's departure.

Having arrived at their destination, they had no means of buying coal or firewood to keep warm in the cold weather, and in this state of extreme poverty Yamazaki fell ill owing to fatigue and malnutrition. He was already affected by tuberculosis. The father of Edward Harrison, the manager of the Yokohama branch of Glover & Co., known as Glover's right-hand man, could not just stand by and let them suffer, so he offered them £25 a month. It was not only Harrison's father who lent them a helping hand. Hearing about them from Masaru Inoue, Williamson and his wife Emma took Yamazaki into their house and nursed him. They did everything they could to make him comfortable, but it was to no avail and on 26 February 1866 he died of pneumonia in hospital. He was 22 years old. The address on his death certificate reads 'c/o Mr John Jones, 166 Camden Street', and Minami's UCL registration also shows his address as 'c/o Mr Jones house', so at some point they seem to have moved out from the Coopers' at 103 Gower Street.

Hirobumi Itō, who had returned to Japan, learned about Yamazaki's death in a letter from Masaru Inoue. 'Hunger and cold', Inoue wrote, 'and his worry and concern for his country caused him mental exhaustion, and led to his death. It is essential to secure funding before sending students abroad.'[52] This incident highlighted how difficult it was to study abroad: a strong will alone was not enough. Study abroad could bear fruit, and the aspirations of those who participated could be realised, but only with adequate financial support such as that provided by Satsuma. Yamazaki proved by his own death that attempting to go abroad to study illegally was to risk one's life.

Yamazaki was buried on Saturday 3 March 1866 in Brookwood Cemetery, Woking, just outside London. A small article in the local paper announced:

> the death of a young Japanese officer who came to this country for educational purposes. Yamasuki [sic] Kosaburo was a native of the province of Nagato, and belonged to the retinue of the Daimyo of that name. His death, at the age of 22 years was caused by consumption. His remains were interred at Woking, the funeral being attended by Professor Williamson and twelve Japanese students of the University College.[53]

Out of those 12 Japanese students, all apart from Masaru Inoue and Minami were from Satsuma. They must have felt mortified at his death, for they had been too busy with their own lives and had failed to save Yamazaki, who had died because he was destitute. They had overcome their feelings of domain rivalry and began to think in terms of the whole nation, mourning the death of a compatriot. They worked hard, sharing the hope that peace and order would soon be re-established in Japan. These men were linked by a common bond, the dream of the restoration of their fatherland.

The young men who died away from home

Brookwood Cemetery was created in 1852 in response to public concern that cemeteries within the city could no longer serve the increase in population. It was managed by the London Necropolis & National Mausoleum Company. The area had been a part of an estate owned by Lord Onslow and was unused heathland known as the Waste of Woking. Some 2,200 acres were bought as common land and 500 acres were marked out for the cemetery. Brookwood Cemetery was opened up for burials in November 1854.

The cemetery is about 35 miles southwest of London, and a special rail service, the London Necropolis Railway, was created at that time for mourners and coffins. A dedicated station was built just next to Waterloo Station, with two more at the cemetery: one at the north end for non-conformists, and one at the south end for Anglicans. The cemetery preserves a densely wooded natural landscape even today, and has the feel of its old name, 'Brookwood Heath'. According to the map of the cemetery at the time of its opening, Yamazaki's grave can be found by following St Augustine's Avenue, which runs southwards straight from South Station, and turning left at the end (Plot 39). The grave is still there, although the epigraph is weathered and is difficult to read in parts. But the letters YAMAZAKI can be clearly seen. The epigraph is engraved in both Japanese and English. In the centre, it reads 'In Memory of YAMAZAKI of Japan Naval officer in the service of Prince Chosiu who departed this life 3rd March 1866 aged 22 years. This stone is erected by his fellow countrymen'. It would appear that the Japanese inscription was added later.

At the time of Yamazaki's death, the south side of the cemetery was designated for Anglicans. So his burial in this part of the cemetery was perhaps an expression of thoughtfulness by his English friends for his untimely death and respect for his fatherland, Japan. Williamson and his wife Emma must have been involved in making the arrangements.

Three more unfortunate Japanese who died in London were buried close to Yamazaki's grave over the next few years (Fig. 27). The gravestone of Jirō Arifuku, a retainer from Tokuyama, a sub-fief of Chōshū, stands behind Yamazaki's. He was the commanding officer of a musket troop, and was one of the first brave soldiers to invade Osaka Castle during the Boshin War of 1868–9. He accompanied Motoisa Mōri, the successor to the lord of Tokuyama, who came to study in England. They arrived in London in April 1868, but Arifuku died of illness soon after, at 50 Grosvenor Road, Highbury New Park, on 13 August. He was 22 years old. He was buried on the following day and the inscription on his gravestone states that it was built according to Motoisa Mōri's instructions.

On the right side of Arifuku's grave lies the coffin-shaped grave of Morito Fukuoka, from Tosa. It is noticeable that the epigraph is only in English with a quotation from the Gospel of St Matthew. He was a son of Kunai Fukuoka, the chief councillor of Tosa, who belonged to the domain's liberal group, and tried his utmost to reform Tosa's policies at the end of the Edo period. Morito Fukuoka, on the order of his domain, came to England to study in November 1871 with Yōtarō Iga, lord of Sukumo, Tosa. He was afflicted with tuberculosis and died on 3 March

Fig. 27 Brookwood Cemetery: graves of four Japanese students who died in London. Courtesy of Nobutaka Sato.

1873 at his lodgings at 37 King Henry's Road, Hampstead. Williamson's house in Fellows Road was a stone's throw away, on the south side of Adelaide Road. Fukuoka was buried on 5 March and the inscription 'He loved and earnestly sought the truth of religion' tells us that he was an ardent Christian seeker.

Kyūhei Fukuro's gravestone, very similar to that of Arifuku, stands to the right of Fukuoka's. He was a younger brother of Seishū Koga, who was a retainer of the Taku family of Saga. He was a highly gifted young man who had learned English from Guido Verbeck, a Dutch-American missionary, in Nagasaki. The Saga clan decided to send several students abroad, and Fukuro was selected together with Torajirō Shinami. They left for Prussia in October 1871. While studying in Berlin Fukuro contracted tuberculosis and had to give up his studies and go back to Japan. However, he died at 28 Northumberland Place in London on 2 November 1873, without managing to reach home. He was 24 years old. His burial was carried out two days later on 4 November. On his gravestone was inscribed 'This monument is erected by his sorrowing friends as a tribute to his worthy and industrious character'.

According to the records of the London Necropolis & National Mausoleum Company, the gravestones of all four men were designated as 'first class, private grave', and each cost £2 10s. The funeral costs were £21 8s for Yamazaki, £19 9s for Fukuro, £12 14s for Fukuoka, and £10 for Arifuku. Their coffins were transported from London to the South Station of the Brookwood Cemetery, and their sombre, solemn burials must have been carried out by a priest of the Anglican Church in the cemetery, attended by their Japanese friends and those English people who had some connection with them.

It was on 11 August 1872 that the first Japanese minister plenipotentiary to Britain, Munenori Terashima, took office at 9 Upper Belgrave Street in a quiet residential area northeast of Victoria Station, so he might well have attended the burials of Fukuoka and Fukuro. Terashima had met Williamson during his first visit to London in 1862, as one of the supervising officers of the Satsuma students. He was aware how Yamazaki had died, and the tragedies of these young men's deaths in a foreign land must have been close to his heart. He left London on 27 August 1873.

Studying abroad with state funds

On his appointment, Terashima was instructed to investigate how Japanese students abroad were living, and he was given authority to send back home those who were unfit. He was working closely with Hirobumi Itō, one of the vice-ambassadors of the Iwakura Mission, who was visiting Britain at that time. Terashima reached the conclusion that there was an urgent need to reorganise Japanese students' study overseas with discipline and order. On 28 November 1873 he dispatched a document entitled 'Proposal for Rules and Regulations for Study Overseas'. Itō also sent written statements regarding study abroad to Takatō Ōki, head of the Education Ministry, and to Kaoru Inoue. In this document, Itō mentioned Charles Graham and wrote:

> Charles Graham, an academic in London, who has been taking good care of our students in his capacity as a teacher, had noticed their difficulties with concern and has given me a paper produced on the basis of his knowledge. He thinks we need to make a 'clean start', so that the students can be of use to the country on a practical level. His arguments might at times sound speculative, but I completely agree with his main points. I have therefore translated his paper and send it to you. I hope it will be useful as reference.[54]

Both Itō and Graham thought that with things as they were, whether students succeeded in their studies or not was a matter of luck. Little would come of their work unless the students were strictly selected according to their intellectual gifts and their character. Graham, who had been strongly influenced by Williamson's teaching, had considerable experience, having taught the Satsuma and other Japanese students. He wanted those who would be influential for the future of Japan to fully understand the spirit of practical science. For this to be achieved, it was essential, he thought, that highly intelligent students should be sent to UCL in greater numbers.

On the basis of the views of Terashima, Itō, Graham and Arinori Mori, the first Japanese minister to the United States, the new government issued the revised 'Rules for Overseas Studies' on 18 March 1873, so a system of government-sponsored study abroad was established. It is no exaggeration to say that Japanese government policy for the overseas studies after the Meiji Restoration was born from the experiences of these early travellers to Britain from Satsuma and Chōshū. The bitter regret for those who died without finishing their studies must have thrown a shadow over those who had shared their lives in London. In this context the Brookwood Cemetery was to become a place remembered by the Japanese as a focal point of the first students who came to London with the hope of contributing to the modernisation of Japan, but in all the turbulent history that followed, 'Brookwood' gradually became forgotten.

The supervising officers of the Satsuma group return home

Now our story goes back to two months before Yamazaki's burial at Brookwood Cemetery. Four men had accompanied the Satsuma students with the aim of making arrangements for their studies and also to investigate the situation in Europe. Three of them, Hisanobu Niiro, Tomoatsu Godai and Takayuki Hori, left for Japan on 31 January 1866. Before their departure they made a renewed request to Williamson to guide their students in their education and other aspects of their lives abroad, and exchanged an agreement. Deciding to spend the last days before their departure in Paris, they had discussions with the French nobleman Charles Comte de Montblanc. This led to a memorandum to establish a trading agreement with Belgium, on 6 February 1867. They finally set sail from Marseilles on 11 February.

The last of the four, Munenori Terashima, was engaged in negotiations with the British Foreign Office. From late March 1866, he had three meetings with the Foreign Secretary, the Earl of Clarendon, requesting the British government's support for Japan's political reforms. Munenori Terashima judged that he had managed a certain measure of success and returned three months later, sailing from Marseilles and taking with him one of the students, Hisanari Murahashi.

An international outlook born of the European experience

Summer 1866. Everybody in London was talking about the Austro-Prussian War. It had started with a dispute between Prussia and Austria over the administration of Schleswig-Holstein, an inevitable conflict in the process of German unification. It began with the Prussian army moving south in June and destroying Austrian army units whenever they met, using modern equipment and superior tactics. By July the outcome was obvious. The Peace of Prague was signed between the Kingdom of Prussia and the Austrian Empire on 23 August 1866. The Prussian victory was much discussed among the students in UCL. Britain, which had been keeping an eye on French activity on the continent after the defeat of Russia in the Crimea, now had to shift its European policy, in response to the Prussian victory over an Austria that had previously been seen as the most powerful state on the continent.

While the war was going on, examinations finished and the summer vacation began. The Satsuma students, who had been experiencing financial difficulties since funds from their domain had ceased to arrive as often as expected, decided that half of them should return home. Moriaki Asakura and Hiroyasu Nakamura had left for Paris to study French at the end of the previous year; of the 12 remaining students, five – Tokinari Nagoya, Ainoshin Tōgō, Yaichi Takami, Shinshirō Machida and Seizō Machida – now decided to return home. Nagoya, Tōgō, Takami and Shinshirō Machida left London on 22 June, and Seizō Machida left from Marseilles at the beginning of August, having spent some time in Paris staying *chez* Montblanc.

Of those who were to stay on in Britain, Hisanari Machida, being in charge of student affairs, remained in London. Kanae Nagasawa continued his work and study in Scotland. The other five – Yoshinari Hatakeyama, Arinori Mori, Naonobu Sameshima, Kiyonari Yoshida and Junzō Matsumura – decided to visit several countries in Europe. Their main aim was to see the state of affairs after the Austro-Prussian War with their own eyes, and the summer vacation provided a good opportunity. Not only Williamson and Emma, but also other intellectuals from Scotland, including Oliphant and Grover, offered assistance to make their expeditions possible.

Arinori Mori had written to his elder brother in Japan on 20 October of the previous year:

> Without seeing the world once it is impossible for us to achieve any great task, I think. Many things are still unclear to me, but since I have come here, to my surprise, my spirit has changed considerably. I think it is vital to study others, and I have been making constant efforts to wash away my previous, muddied thoughts.[55]

He seems to have been genuinely surprised at the changes occurring in himself since he arrived in Britain, and he was determined to improve himself by getting rid of feudal, old-fashioned ideas. In a later letter, dated 19 January 1866, in response to his own question on how one could acquire the strength to rebuild a country, he wrote that going around the world and closely observing other systems and structures of states, the people and their customs were essential preparations for the

Fig. 28 Arinori Mori while staying in Russia, 1866. Courtesy of Satsuma Students Museum, Kagoshima.

great task that lay ahead. Mori believed that he had to reform himself before he could reform Japan. In a scientific and empirical atmosphere, and surrounded by many able academics and kind friends, he was receiving a rigorous, practical education.

With a strong sense of purpose, Mori and Matsumura left London for Russia (Fig. 28), Sameshima and Yoshida went to the United States, and Hatakeyama to France. Their trips were all very profitable and fruitful. Returning to London after a month in Russia, Mori again wrote to his elder brother on 4 September:

> Recently we Japanese have begun to gain knowledge of foreign countries and an increasing number of students are involved in Western studies. However, the majority of people are interested only in the end products (arts and technology); they remain ignorant of the learning that forms the basis of the country.[56]

By the word 'basis' Mori meant law. He considered law to be the backbone of a country, and unless law was clearly established there was no hope of governing a country where people would be safe. He later realised that what was really fundamental was not law itself, but what underpins law, namely a country's ethos and morality. Thus Mori began his journey to find what lay at the foundation of this 'ethos and morality', in other words 'the quintessence of the West'.

Mori and Junzō Matsumura came back from Russia convinced that it was a lawless, underdeveloped country ignorant of international morality. Sameshima and Yoshida, on the other hand, praised American democratic politics; and Hatakeyama was critical of the imperialistic policies of Napoleon III. The students came to the view that the relative merits of countries should be assessed on the basis of whether those countries followed principles of international morality or not, and it was around this time that they began forming their international perspective. Evidently their views were influenced by the humanist Oliphant and the cosmopolitan Williamson.

Towards the unity of science and technology

The summer vacation ended and the second year of study for the Satsuma students began in October 1866. Hatakeyama, Mori, Sameshima, Yoshida and Matsumura all decided to take a physics laboratory course taught by George Carey Foster, along with Williamson's analytical chemistry, and they each paid £9 9s. We have mentioned Foster a number of times already; what follows is a description of his academic career.

Having worked as Williamson's assistant for several years, Foster went to Ghent University in Belgium in 1858 and studied under the German chemist Friedrich Kekulé, a close friend of Williamson. He then continued his research in Paris and Heidelberg, and in 1862 was appointed Professor of Natural Philosophy at Anderson's University in Glasgow. He was one of Williamson's most highly regarded students. He wanted to establish a course in practical physics, of a kind that did not yet exist in Britain. Williamson, who supported Foster's ambition, recommended him for the post of Professor of Experimental Physics at UCL, a post that was newly established in 1865. Returning to UCL, Foster created the Department of Physics, and was involved in teaching for the next 33 years until 1898. He served as the first Principal of UCL from 1900 till 1904.

Foster accompanied the Satsuma students on their visit to the Britannia Iron Works in Bedford. He was Professor at Anderson's

University at the time, but in the article in the *Bedfordshire Times* he is mistakenly referred to as 'the Professor of Natural Philosophy at Glasgow University'.

In 1866, encouraged by the experience of the Bedford visit, Williamson introduced factory visits as a formal part of the curriculum. Witnessing the Satsuma students' wildly enthusiastic response to seeing how science was actually used in machinery and technology must have been a stimulating experience. It must have confirmed his belief that technology could only really be taught on the factory floor. Williamson's policy of integrating science and technology was inherited by his students. Foster's practical physics course and Graham's chemical technology course are fine examples of the fruit of Williamson's teaching. Graham's course was later known as applied chemistry. Regarding the choice of subjects for their second year, the Satsuma students had different ideas from Graham, who was their academic mentor, but in the end they decided to follow his advice, opting for a science subject first and a more technically oriented course second. They needed thorough knowledge of applied science before putting it into practice.

In the academic year starting October 1866 there were five students from Satsuma, and just Masaru Inoue from Chōshū. Minami was attending Williamson's applied chemistry lectures after Yamazaki's death, but had moved on to Woolwich where he was receiving military pre-training in a private institution. However, having no more financial support, he had no choice but to return to Japan in the autumn. Masaru Inoue's work at UCL went well. He studied mathematical physics and geological mineralogy, and in the summer of 1867 went to Newcastle to learn skills related to mining and the railways. Following Williamson's teaching, he was working hard to acquire techniques of how to apply science that would be useful back in Japan.

The realities of international relations

From the end of 1866 and during the following year British society was moving in a new direction. Movements for workers' rights began, and the Reform League, whose president was the barrister Edmund Beales, was pressing for manhood suffrage by stirring up the masses and skilled workers. John Bright, an MP who advocated free trade, supported the Liberal leader Gladstone, and worked towards the unionisation of the working class. The Second Reform Act, now often regarded as the most significant reform in the era of progress and prosperity, was passed by

Parliament in August 1867. Many urban working-class people gained the right to vote, although this was still based on the ownership of property. Popular democracy had arrived. The first volume of Marx's *Das Kapital*, which was to provide the theoretical basis of the labour movement, was also published in this year, and the second General Congress of the International Workingmen's Association was held in Lausanne in September.

On 1 April 1867, the International Exposition opened at the Champ de Mars in Paris. This was the grandest of all the world's fairs up to that date. Napoleon III, who had a very active foreign policy, had encouraged not only European countries but also less developed countries in the Middle East, the Far East and South America to participate. Japan was one of the countries to respond positively. A space for Japan was designated on the site, and there were cultural exhibits from Satsuma and Saga. Many domains also sent their officials, and as a result numbers of Japanese travellers to Europe increased. The Satsuma students found some free time during their studies and managed to get to Paris. They had meetings with Japanese delegates and made contacts with many people from different countries. This was an opportunity to experience the reality of international relations, something that they could not learn at university. On 12 May, Hisanari Machida, who had been in charge of student affairs in London, left for Japan from Marseilles with the Satsuma delegation to the Exposition.

Taking a critical look at the West

While all this was going on, the situation in Japan was becoming critical. The desire to restore imperial rule was changing into an anti-shogunate movement. The departure of Hisanari Machida triggered some feelings of uncertainty among the remaining Satsuma students. Some could see no good reason to continue their studies at university and felt that it would be better to go back home and do what they could to save Japan. The person who guided them through their difficulties was the MP Laurence Oliphant, who often invited them to his house and kept them informed about international developments. He also tried to persuade them to find a way to save their country through faith, introducing them to the Anglo-American preacher Thomas Lake Harris (1823–1906), whose teachings Oliphant had embraced.

On 12 May, the same day that Hisanari Machida set sail from Marseilles, Oliphant introduced the five Satsuma students to the MP

John Bright. Despite an age gap, Oliphant and Bright were good friends. Bright wrote in his diary:

> To dinner with Laurence Oliphant, MP, near Clarence Gate. Met five young men from Japan, students here, and passed a most pleasant evening with them. They are robust, and very intelligent, scarcely so tall as Englishmen, but strong in build, and with heads of more than average breadth and power. They have the 'eastern' eyes, rather high cheek-bones, and are slightly dark complexioned, tho' one of them is lighter than many Englishmen, and the hands of one of them are quite as white as is common here … These young gentlemen are gentlemen in manner, and in conduct and thought, and would bear themselves becomingly in any English society.[57]

When Bright heard the students talking about the idea of saving their country based on Harris's ideas of faith, he wondered whether they really understood Christianity. About a month later, on 23 June, Oliphant invited Arinori Mori, Naonobu Sameshima and Yoshimoto Hanabusa, a visiting student from the Okayama domain, to his house in Regent's Park. According to Hanabusa, Oliphant, in the relaxed atmosphere after dinner, talked passionately:

> These days, world powers are just seeking profit for themselves and do not admit to wrongdoing. In the end they will destroy themselves. Britain and France are enjoying momentary prosperity and the people, both high and low, have become greedy; they are suffering from the 'disease of luxury', for which there is no cure. There are some good countries left in Europe but they too are not free from this disease. They may look strong, but their spirit is such that they can do nothing.[58]

Here we can clearly see Oliphant's self-examination and his criticism of civilisation, of the imperialism of Europe and America, seeking profit no matter what. He saw it as a 'disease of luxury', a 'disease of civilisation'. The only way to save Japan in all its purity, a country not yet affected by such diseases, was, he said, to maintain regard for loyalty and humility, and to conduct diplomacy based on international moral grounds. The students were drawn to his advice, and decided to send an official letter to the leaders of the Satsuma domain, dated 10 July 1867:

At the beginning of our time in Britain, we were simply amazed by everything we saw, without really understanding what it meant. As time went by, we gradually realised that there are things we should avoid [copying]. We are fortunate to have met a good friend who has told us in detail of the realities of Europe and America, and we now understand that there are only a few things we should learn and adopt, and many other things that we should avoid. He has explained that although the position of the British government might appear to be fair on the surface, it is merely a front and in reality they are high-handed and autocratic. We could not but fully agree with him. It is the characteristic of European countries and America to think of nothing but their own profit, exploit other countries, make alliances with the powerful, and reject the weak.[59]

Under Oliphant's influence, the students were beginning to develop a critical sense. Paradoxically, this is one indication that they were coming close to understanding the 'quintessence of the West'.

Six Satsuma students leave for America

The remaining six Satsuma students, including Kanae Nagasawa in Scotland, were no longer receiving financial support from home despite repeated requests sent through the domain's mission in Paris, and it looked as if they had been completely forgotten. Indeed, one of the reasons that they sent the letter quoted above was to remind Satsuma of their existence. The only way they could continue their studies was to earn money themselves.

Their lack of funds, combined with their faith in Harris's teaching, led them to decide to travel to America. Williamson, Graham, Foster and the other academics who had been assisting them at UCL were completely opposed to their decision, because they apparently regarded Harris as a mad fantasist. At first the Satsuma students hesitated, but when they heard that Oliphant was going to join Harris's spiritual community, the Brotherhood of the New Life, in upstate New York, they decided to go. In the middle of August, within a month of Oliphant's departure for America, the six Satsuma students bade farewell to the Williamsons and other friends and left London.

The demands of the time

Soon after the Satsuma students left Britain, Satsuma, Chōshū and Hiroshima domains entered into an alliance to raise an army to defeat the *bakufu*. On 8 November 1868, Satsuma and Chōshū received the secret imperial command to challenge the shogunate and the following day, Yoshinobu Tokugawa, the fifteenth Shogun, ceded power to the emperor. Kogorō Katsura (aka Takayoshi Kido) of Chōshū, in a letter written to Yasushirō Kawase, who had just arrived in Britain, wrote that a great revolution was at hand, which would demonstrate to the world the ideal of a united imperial Japan and create its foundations. It would be the task of those Japanese who were abroad to explain the situation to the European powers, he said, and added: 'The *daimyō* had ordered Yakichi Nomura (Masaru Inoue) to return home but we have not heard from him, so everyone is concerned about him. Please persuade him to come back at the earliest opportunity.'[60]

Masaru Inoue and Yōzō Yamao, who were living in Britain and had opportunities to learn technologies and the spirit of Western civilisation, were expected to return home as soon as possible and to become instruments of modernisation of their fatherland Japan. Masaru Inoue received Katsura's letter on 30 November and wrote back to him on 10 December:

> I am well aware that my Lord has ordered to me to return home, and I too have been hoping to return home as soon as possible; but I have yet to complete the task that was given me, so I am unable to obey. May I be granted ten more months' leave? If I return without completing what I have set myself to learn, the knowledge I have already gained with considerable hardship will be of no use. Please intercede on my behalf.[61]

He added that Yamao, studying in a shipyard in Glasgow, would probably share his view. They had given their word of honour to become 'living machines', and they did not want to go home without having done so. In later years Masaru Inoue, looking back on his period of study in England, was full of regret that he was forced to obey the order and break off his studies: 'Heaven betrays man and events did not go according to one's desires; I returned half-way through my apprenticeship.' He had intended to master Western technology and return as an accomplished engineer. As a technician, from his own pragmatic point of view, Masaru Inoue directly linked his own progress as an engineer to the goal of national reform.

Yamao, on the other hand, saw Japan's modernisation as an amalgam of technological and political reform. Many Japanese young men who studied abroad realised that the modernisation of their country was not simply a matter of industrial, military and technological progress, but involved a cultural change in the people themselves. They had gone all the way to Europe with an acute sense of crisis between Japan and the outside world, and they had discovered a view of humanity, ethics and society totally different from those in the East. There were some who felt that their task was to understand the essence of the mentality that underlay Western civilisation, absorb it, and 'civilise' themselves. They believed that only after having become civilised themselves, through gaining both technology and knowledge, would they be truly able to help in the modernisation of Japan.

Most of the early travellers who left Japan illegally thought like this. Their sense of urgency, of being always close to death, made them feel they had to change themselves, but it also implanted in them a clear sense of nationhood. With their widened horizons, they could see the need for reform, both of their country and their people, and this became, along with the knowledge they acquired and technology they learned about in Britain, a significant dynamic force behind the formation of the new Japan after the Meiji Restoration.

Masaru Inoue and Yamao's return home

Masaru Inoue was awarded a distinction (third in his class) in the public examination in geology in 1866–7, and received a Certificate of Honour. The course he took was taught by John Morris, who had started his teaching carrier at UCL in 1853. Morris was initially a pharmaceutical chemist but changed to geology and was well known for his innovative method of teaching. He was one of the first people to introduce field trips as a part of his course, and he also created a geology museum.

Having achieved distinguished results in the examination, Masaru Inoue went to Newcastle to be trained in mining. He requested via Katsura that his *daimyō* grant ten more months of leave, as he reckoned that it would take at least one year to be properly trained in mining technology; but his request was refused and he received an order to return home without delay, together with Yamao.

On 19 June 1868 Motoiki Mōri (aged 18), heir apparent of Tokuyama, a sub-fief of Chōshū, arrived in London, bringing with him five retainers, Naosuke Ōno (28), Jirō Arifuku (22), Ryōzō Ikeda (33), Minato Itō (31) and Teiichirō Endō (28). Motoiki Mōri was scheduled to study artillery. Along with Yamao, who had returned to London from Glasgow ready to travel back to Japan, Masaru Inoue must have gone to visit him. As already recorded, one of his group, Jirō Arifuku, died suddenly and was buried at Brookwood Cemetery. The inscription on his gravestone was written by his friend Naosuke Ōno. Ōno studied economics in London, went home in 1870 and later became director general of the banking bureau in the Ministry of Finance.

Masaru Inoue and Yamao must have attended Arifuku's burial and paid their respects at the grave of their friend Yamazaki, reporting that they had to return home. They must have also promised to return as 'living machines' and do their utmost for the modernisation of Japan. Two months later, Masaru Inoue and Yamao left London. They had been in Britain for five years. Saying his farewell at 12 Fellows Road, where he had been looked after so well in both private and public matters by Williamson and his wife Emma, Masaru Inoue presented a tapestry entitled *British Butterflies*, designed by William Morris, to express his gratitude.

Masaru Inoue and Yamao set foot again in Yokohama on the evening of 30 December 1868. Japan was just about to wake to a new dawn – the 'Meiji'.

6

Bridge to Japan's modernisation

After all the Japanese students under Williamson's care had left, his life became much quieter. Some time later, a Japanese writing case arrived as a parting present from the Chōshū students. Williamson and his wife cherished it as a memento. Not only had the experience of teaching the Japanese students enriched Williamson's experience of education but it also brought a new dimension to his research. Around this time Williamson began again to challenge the scepticism with which British chemists regarded the theory of atoms.

The spread of pure science

At one scientific meeting Williamson, who had always been a defender of the atomic theory, gave a lecture titled 'On the Atomic Theory' which was published in the *Journal of the Chemical Society* in January 1869. Many people listened to his lecture with great attention and his theory attracted increasing interest from researchers. After the summer vacation, further meetings were held to discuss the matter.

Two years earlier, in 1867, William Thomson, a physicist and Professor of Natural Philosophy at Glasgow University, had suggested in his paper, 'On Vortex Atoms', that the atom was a vortex motion in a perfect fluid, and this had brought a considerable response. According to his theory, matter, light and electricity were considered as movements in a fluid. Many physicists and chemists, still supporting Dalton's concept of atoms as static particles, showed little interest. Williamson argued strongly in favour of following the evidence rather than unsubstantiated theories, and he wrote at the conclusion of 'On the Atomic Theory':

> They may be vortices, such as Thomson has spoken of; they may be
> little hard indivisible particles of regular or irregular form … In

conclusion I must say that the vast body of evidence of the most various kinds, and from the most various sources, all pointing to the one central idea of atoms, does seem to me a truly admirable result of human industry and thought. Our atomic theory is the consistent general expression of all the best known and best arranged facts of the science, and certainly it is the very life of chemistry.[62]

Williamson's atomic theory, which he called 'dynamic atomism', had a significant influence on research in chemistry and physics in later years.

Williamson was next involved in an organisational reform of UCL. He aimed to make the science sections independent of the Faculty of Arts and Laws in order to gather the best scientists at UCL, a move that was also made in response to the general increase in demand for science education. The Council was persuaded by his plan for reform, and in 1870 UCL established its Faculty of Science. Williamson became the first chairman of the Faculty and he delivered his inaugural lecture, titled 'A Plea for Pure Science':

Now, science has a powerful influence on the business of life ... A correct appreciation of the conditions requisite for theory and practice respectively, will suffice to show the natural order of a general system of education ... The department of Learning denoted by the word Science, is dignified by the academic title of Faculty without being severed from kindred subjects, with which many good offices are interchanged ... Thus, the lectures on Physics and on Chemistry afford verbal descriptions of things or of phenomena, accompanied, in many cases, by an examination of the things described. The relations of phenomena to one another are also frequently illustrated by experiment, as well as described in general terms by a law. In like manner, instruction in Geology, Botany, Zoology, Physiology, &c., is illustrated by carefully selected specimens or experiments ... The great aim and object of science is to systematize our knowledge; and the discovery of an idea which helps to arrange any considerable number of facts, in such a manner as to facilitate their apprehension, is the highest result of scientific work.[63]

In the latter half of his lecture he expressed his limitless trust in human progress and development, and voiced his positive views on the theory of natural selection:

From time to time an individual appears possessing the very excellences of his parents in a still greater degree than them: his existence is the germ of progress, and his success in the struggle for subsistence is the process which constitutes the development of progress.[64]

With praise, he called this law, which was representative of the spirit of the era, 'the Law of Progress'. In conclusion Williamson stated the importance of 'the recognition by the State of the Pure Sciences as an essential element of national greatness and progress'[65] and made a plea for the spread of pure sciences in education nationwide, particularly in universities. Williamson then put his ideals into practice. He set up a new system in the teaching of engineering by introducing experiments as a part of the course, not only in his university but also as part of a national curriculum. He also worked hard towards the establishment of degrees in sciences in UCL. He was determined to instil science in national education, and spared no effort in working towards this goal.

Results of practical education

At precisely this time, in 1871, a Japanese student arrived at the newly established Science Faculty at UCL. His name was Taizō Masaki (Fig. 29), from Chōshū, and he had been sent by the Japanese Mint on a government scholarship. In 1868 imperial rule had been restored and the Meiji government, in which Satsuma and Chōshū occupied important positions, was established. After the end of the Boshin Civil War, the feudal lords relinquished their status as local rulers, and returned their authority over lands and their populations to the throne (known as the 'Return of the Registers'). This brought an end to the feudal system, and the effort to build the new nation began. In July of that year a major reform of regulations for governmental organisations was implemented. The Board of Religion and the Executive Board were both directly answerable to the emperor, with six ministries under the latter: Home Affairs, Finance, Military Affairs, Justice, the Imperial Household and Foreign Affairs. With this reform the new government took a significant step forward in bureaucratic organisation and the centralisation of power.

The government established the Mint under the Ministry of Finance and appointed Kaoru Inoue to run it. As part of the modernisation, Inoue employed foreign engineers and in July 1870 he proposed to send

Fig. 29   Taizō Masaki. Courtesy of Tokyo Institute of Technology.

students to Britain as an investment in human resources. The proposal was accepted, and in March of the following year seven students including Hyakutarō Toyahara and Taizō Masaki were sent to London to learn the technologies necessary for the Mint.

Toyohara and Masaki entered UCL and took Williamson's analytical chemistry and Graham's practical chemistry courses. Graham taught with Williamson as an assistant professor of chemistry between 1873 and 1878, and when chemical engineering was split from analytical chemistry, Graham became its first professor. The teaching in the newly established Faculty of Science must have been wonderfully stimulating for these Japanese students. Kaoru Inoue and his successor at the Mint, Kinsuke Endō, had recommended that newly arrived students take these courses.

To digress for a moment, after Masaki returned to Japan in 1874 he taught chemistry for two years as an assistant lecturer at the Kaisei

School, which was the precursor of the University of Tokyo. Then in 1876 he was sent back to Britain by the Ministry of Education to investigate and assess the conditions of Japanese students studying there.

In the autumn of 1878, while at the University of Edinburgh, Masaki was introduced by Fleeming Jenkin (1833–1885), the Professor of Chemistry, to a young Scotsman, Robert Louis Stevenson (1850–1894), who had just published *An Inland Voyage* based on a canoe voyage in Belgium and France. Stevenson's father was a leading lighthouse engineer who also taught at the university. Stevenson himself had studied engineering, and looked up to Professor Jenkin as a mentor. He was attracted to writers such as Victor Hugo in France, and Walt Whitman in America, and dreamed of becoming a writer of the romantic school, reflecting high ideals. When Masaki first met Stevenson, he told him many stories about his own spiritual master, Shōin Yoshida (1830–1859; aka Torajirō Yoshida, Fig. 30), and Stevenson was particularly drawn to the tale of Yoshida's attempt to steal abroad and his subsequent failure and imprisonment. Two years later, in 1880, he published an essay, 'Yoshida Torajirō' (later collected in *Familiar Studies of Men and Books*), which is the first biography of the subject written by a foreigner. Stevenson praised Shōin Yoshida's courage in attempting the illegal trip abroad, and wrote, 'For their act was unprecedented; it was criminal; and it was to take them beyond the pale of humanity into a land of devils.'[66] The five Chōshū students had been strongly influenced by Shōin Yoshida's courage.

On his return to Japan Masaki, as the first president of the Tokyo Vocational School (the present-day Tokyo Institute of Technology), was responsible for the teaching of technological skills, another example of the impact of Williamson's practical education.

The teachers who came from Britain

In Japan many bureaucratic reforms followed the Meiji Restoration and a Ministry of Education was established under the Executive. Then the Ministry for Home Affairs was merged with the Ministry of Finance. Mining and railways, originally under the Ministry of Home Affairs, were moved to the Ministry of Industry, which had been created the year before. The original Chōshū Five found many opportunities to serve in this newly established ministry. Hirobumi Itō became Minister of Industry, Yōzō Yamao was in charge of industry and surveying, and Masaru Inoue became head of mining and railways. Kaoru Inoue became

Fig. 30   Shōin Yoshida. Courtesy of Yamaguchi Prefectural Archive.

Minister of Finance, and Kinsuke Endō was the head of the Mint. All of them made significant contributions using their specialised knowledge and technological understanding in the service of modernising Japan.

Following these internal reforms, Japan decided to send a diplomatic mission to Europe and America led by senior statesmen. The mission was headed by Tomomi Iwakura in the role of extraordinary and plenipotentiary ambassador, and four vice-ambassadors were appointed: Counsellor Takayoshi Kido, Minister of Finance Toshimichi Ōkubo, Minister of Industry Hirobumi Itō and Vice-minister of Foreign Affairs Masuka Yamaguchi. One of the aims of the mission was to start preliminary renegotiation of the unequal treaties Japan had signed with foreign powers in an attempt to avoid being colonised, and to investigate the systems and structures of the United States and European countries. Forty-three students were added to the mission and altogether 107 people left Yokohama on 23 December 1871. They arrived in San Francisco, their first port of call, on 15 January 1872, and seven months later, on 17 August, they arrived in London, their second port of call.

Itō had consulted with Yamao before their departure, and they had agreed to establish a College of Civil Engineering as part of their investment in human resources at the Ministry of Industry. Itō went to see Hugh Matheson of Jardine Matheson, who had looked after him when he was a student in London, and requested his assistance in selecting teachers to work in Japan. After consulting with Lewis D.B. Gordon and William J.M. Rankine, both professors of engineering at the University of Glasgow, Matheson introduced Itō to a young man called Henry Dyer (1848–1918). Itō immediately decided to invite Dyer to be the principal engineering professor at the college that was about to be established. Dyer, following Itō's instructions, began selecting teachers to go with him. It seems likely that the selection was influenced by Dyer's teacher Professor Rankine and William Thomson, who was Professor of Physics. Among those who were selected, all former students of Professor Thomson, were William Edward Ayrton (1847–1908), an electrical engineer, and Edward Divers (1837–1912), a chemist. Consequently the new College of Civil Engineering's teaching members were all connected with the University of Glasgow. The nine teachers arrived together at Yokohama in June 1873.

Matheson must have asked Williamson's views on this selection of teachers, particularly on William Ayrton, a former student of his. Ayrton entered UCL in 1864, studied mathematics and graduated in 1867, so he overlapped with the Satsuma and Chōshū students. He was the same age as Arinori Mori. After his graduation, Ayrton went to Glasgow and studied physics under Professor Thomson. Ayrton's attitude towards research clearly reflects Williamson's ideal of the merging of chemistry and physics. After his studies Ayrton first went to India in the service of the Indian Government Telegraph Department and returned in 1872 to work for the Great Western Railway in Scotland. There his old teacher Professor Thomson, and Professor Jenkin of Edinburgh, approached him with the idea of going to Japan to teach. He married just before his departure, and his wife Matilda, who had studied medicine at Edinburgh and was a pioneer female doctor in Britain, went with him. Ayrton was an authority in electrical and lighting engineering and taught Saburō Shida, who later became the first professor of electrical engineering in Japan. Ayrton stressed the importance of experiments and always demanded that his students do some meteorological forecasting before he lectured on thermometry. His wife opened a school for midwives in Tokyo and encouraged the study of obstetrics. The contribution of the Ayrtons to the development of science in Japan was highly significant. In 1878 they returned to Britain and he taught at the City & Guilds' Finsbury College and Central College in South Kensington. He died in 1908 at the age of 61.

The establishment of Tokyo Kaisei School

While the Iwakura Mission was visiting the United States and Europe, it was aided by the young men once taught by Williamson. Naonobu Sameshima was one of the first Japanese diplomats and had been serving as the country's minister in Paris since 1871. There he took care of students from Japan and was also engaged in selecting foreign experts to go and work in Japan. Arinori Mori was in Washington as the Japanese minister to the United States and he was involved in tasks similar to Sameshima's. Munenori Terashima was the first minister to Great Britain and took office in 1872. He was very active, travelling all over Europe.

Yoshinari Hatakeyama, who graduated from Rutgers University in New Jersey in 1871, joined the mission as third secretary, and studied education systems in Europe and the US. In December 1873 he became the first principal of the Kaisei School, the only institution of higher education in Japan at the time (Fig. 31). It was renamed Tokyo Kaisei School in May 1874, and in September of that year started to offer specialised courses. Departments of law, chemistry and engineering were established, marking the beginning of higher education comparable to that in the West. Under Hatakeyama's leadership, highly trained

Fig. 31 Tokyo Kaisei School around the time of its opening in 1871. Courtesy of National Diet Library, Tokyo.

lecturers were sought out: from Britain came William E. Grigsby for law, Robert William Atkinson for chemistry and Robert H. Smith for mechanical engineering. It is probable that Hatakeyama consulted Williamson about who to select. In 1873 Williamson became foreign secretary of the Royal Society, responsible for the society's external contacts. He held the office the next 16 years. He also became a member of the Senate of London University.

The College of Civil Engineering under the Ministry of Industry employed foreign teachers, most of them associated with the University of Glasgow, whereas Tokyo Kaisei School had scholars mainly from London University.

Tokyo Kaisei School was at Kanda Nishiki-chō, 3-1. The newly built school was a two-storied, wooden, Western-style house painted white and looked the part. The location was by the Kanda Hitotsubashi Bridge, with the School of Foreign Languages on the other side of the street. A student of that time left a vivid description:

> The School was a two-storied building in the shape of the letter 'H'. Two wings, north and south, faced each other 73 metres apart, and stretched 36 metres from east to west. The building was made of wood and painted white. Going through the gate, there was a small

mound with pine trees, and further in, on a grass-covered mound in the north corner, there was a flagpole with the flag of Kaisei School in red letters on a white background. The flagpole, porter's lodge, gates and fences were all white and looked magnificent. The atmosphere was so pure and clean that we felt inspired.[67]

It was an enormous national project. The area of the school site was about 6,000 m² and it cost 58,000 yen. Hatakeyama saw this school as a national college to educate specialists. When his plan was completed, it consisted of five schools – law, chemistry, engineering, arts and mining, and he aimed to develop it into a university comparable to those in Europe and America. Now this area is occupied by the Gakushi Kaikan, the Universities' Alumni Association Hall, and there is nothing to remind us of the old school.

Atkinson's achievement

Robert William Atkinson came to this brand new white building for the first time in September 1874. Williamson had recommended him very highly and Atkinson took up the post with high ambition to produce good chemists in Japan using the same methods as Williamson. A young man, only 24 years old, from Newcastle, he had studied chemistry at the Royal College of Chemistry and the Royal School of Mines. He was a highly talented individual and had been appointed as a teaching assistant in Williamson's chemistry laboratory at UCL in 1872. For the publication of the third edition of Williamson's textbook *Chemistry for Students*, the editing work fell to Atkinson. At the end of the preface, Williamson expressed his gratitude: 'My friend Atkinson kindly took the trouble to do the editing. I greatly benefited from his useful suggestions for the arrangements of the parts where organic chemical compounds are discussed'.[68]

As requested by Hatakeyama, Atkinson taught analytical chemistry and manufacturing chemistry. In the analytical chemistry course he first taught the basic nature of elements with practical work, and then moved on to quantitative analysis. In the manufacturing chemistry course he taught the uses of coal, the process for manufacturing coal gas and the method of creating aniline from the tar produced during gasification. Hardly any students had ever seen the production in practice, so just as Williamson had done, Atkinson took his students to a gas-making plant.

It was in Yokohama in 1872 that the first gas light appeared in Japan. In Tokyo, gas lamps were lit between Kyōbashi and Shinbashi in 1874. Atkinson, accompanied by Taizō Masaki who was acting as his assistant, took his students to a gas plant in Shinbashi. Looking back on those times, Jōji Sakurai, one of Atkinson's first students, wrote:

> A new well-equipped laboratory was built, and the proper chemistry course with Professor Atkinson started in the seventh year of Meiji (1874). He was to remain in that post until 1881. During the seven years he spent in Japan he encouraged research and development, and rendered distinguished service … I was one of his first students and whenever I look back at the way he guided us towards science with unfailing enthusiasm and fortitude, I am overwhelmed with gratitude.[69]

He lectured many hours each week, taking on the teaching of theoretical chemistry and metallurgy in addition to analytical and practical chemistry. Masuzō Ueno, the author of a short biography of Atkinson, praised his work during these pioneering days of modern chemistry, and wrote: 'The systematic transfer of the knowledge of chemistry to Japan owes everything to Atkinson'.[70]

While working in Japan Atkinson carried out research on brewing, as he was interested in the process of making Japanese *sake*. Williamson had done research on fermentation and his interest might well have influenced Atkinson's choice of subject. Atkinson visited *sake* breweries in Nishinomiya and Itami, and investigated how *sake* was produced. An outline of the results of his research appeared in *Nature* in 1878, and a paper entitled 'The Chemistry of Sake Brewing' was published in the journal of the Faculty of Science, Tokyo University, in 1881. This paper, the first of its kind, was translated into Japanese and published in the same year. It was a clear example of what Williamson had always advocated, namely the fusion of pure and applied science. *Sake*, a unique cultural product of Japan, was analysed using Western scientific methods, and the paper is interesting in the context of comparative culture.

Atkinson also left pioneering results in areas of Japanese culture that had not previously been much studied, such as the special reflections seen in ancient bronze mirrors. He was also, together with Ernest Satow, one of the first mountain climbers in Japan. He returned to Britain in July 1881 before the official end of his contract, and worked as a technical consultant for the coal and iron ore industry in Cardiff. He died at the age of 79, on 10 December 1929. Atkinson taught in Japan for only seven years, but in that short time he introduced modern chemistry, established chemistry education and trained those who could continue his work, all in the footsteps of Williamson. For these achievements he should be remembered.

Studying abroad under the Meiji government

The new Meiji government felt under pressure to review how students were sent abroad from the point of view of students' ability, their health and funding, and it had been in discussions with foreign authorities via the Iwakura Mission. The first students from Chōshū and Satsuma helped to shape government policy. A draft report entitled 'Rules and Regulations for Study Abroad' was published by the Ministry of Education on 18 March 1873. Based on this report, in December the Ministry ordered that all students who were currently abroad should return to Japan. A year later, in December 1874, the Ministry decided on a quota of 30 of the most able students to send abroad. The first group included 11 from the Kaisei School, nine of whom were sent to America: four for law, three for chemistry, two for engineering. Two who were still in their preparatory year were sent to Europe: one to France, and another to Germany to study mining. They left on 31 July 1875 and returned in 1880 after studying abroad for five years.

In June 1876, the Ministry of Education selected another 10 students from the same school and sent them to Britain and France. Three of them were to study law, two chemistry, three engineering, and two physics. They were all young men in their late teens or early twenties. They left on 25 June and returned in 1881. The chemistry students, Jōji Sakurai and Jūgō Sugiura, had already specialised in chemistry at Kaisei School. Sakurai, who studied at UCL under Williamson, described their journey:

> The cohort of the ninth year of Meiji set sail from Yokohama in the early morning of 25 June 1876 on the *Alaska* belonging to an American line. Masaki Taizō was in charge. We travelled to Britain via America. I remember Kaoru Inoue with his wife and daughter; Yoshio Kusaka, Yukinaga Magaki, Kojirō Amano, Naganobu Sasaki and Tamiyoshi Zushi were also on board. The *Alaska* was a paddle steamer of about 2,000 tons, which also had sail. We sailed directly to San Francisco without calling at Honolulu, taking 25 days to cover about 4,700 nautical miles. This means that our average

speed was about eight knots. The American coast-to-coast railroad had been completed only a few years previously and the main cities were already connected by train. We went from San Francisco to Chicago, Niagara, Philadelphia and New York. We had the opportunity to visit the Centennial Exposition, Expo 1876, in Philadelphia. We arrived in London on 18 August, which was, incidentally, my eighteenth birthday.[71]

For Kaoru Inoue, accompanied by his wife and daughter this time, the visit marked 13 years since his illegal voyage to Britain at the end of the Edo period. He was commissioned to stay in Europe for three years for research into economics and finance. While in London he stayed with an economist, and observed how the British industrial economy worked, as well as studying the taxation system. He considered that it was essential to raise the capacity of people and to develop industry in order to achieve a civilised nation. Furthermore he realised that for the true advancement of a nation, military and economic power alone were not enough, and that the trust of the international community played a most significant role. Inoue's idea echoes what Williamson had been trying to advocate and it was an important issue in Japan's modernisation.

7
Towards 'unity out of difference'

In 1878 UCL took an unprecedented step. The Council allowed female students to enter the University with equal status to the male students. H. Hale Bellot, in the official history of the first 100 years of the College, called it 'the most revolutionary development' in the history of UCL.[72] This was a ground-breaking change not only for British universities but also for universities in Europe. In that first year 309 women matriculated, a truly remarkable figure, just short of half the number of male students who entered that year. The London Ladies' Education Association had been demanding that UCL open its doors to women, and Henry Morley, the Professor of English, and Carey Foster, the Professor of Physics, had worked hard for this aim.

In March 1869, Morley and Foster had opened two courses for women – in literature and science – at Beethoven Quartet Rooms in Harley Street. This initiative spread quickly and two pilot science courses were established in UCL by the winter of that same year. Six academics – Williamson, T.A. Hirst for mathematics, J.R. Seeley for Latin, H.C.S. Cassal for French, Morley and Foster – ran courses for women in 1870–1. From early on Williamson was of the opinion that university education should be open to women, so he must have been willingly involved with Foster's revolutionary idea of reforming UCL. It fitted perfectly with Williamson's fundamental belief, 'unity out of difference'. He believed that civilisation would progress and develop in an environment where both men and women enjoyed higher education. Foster and Morley continued their efforts in developing co-education, and on 1 October 1882 a residential hall for female students, College Hall, opened at 1 Byng Place. At first only 10 students came to stay but the number increased year by year and soon a second and then a third hall were built. Byng Place leads into Gower Street on the south side of UCL and is one of the main areas of student life in London.

The Chair of Chemical Technology was established in 1878 and Charles Graham, who had been assistant professor under Williamson, became its first holder. His teaching was given in the same building that chemistry students normally used. Williamson requested that the College build a new chemistry laboratory for his classes and it was agreed that it would be built on the north wing of the College. In 1880 the chemistry students moved to the newly established laboratory.

Under the tutelage of Williamson

It must have been around September 1876 that Jōji Sakurai, a Japanese government scholar, came to see Williamson with his former student, Taizō Masaki. This intelligent-looking young man must have reminded Williamson of the time that he looked after students from Satsuma and Chōshū. Ten years had passed but Williamson still remembered well the expressions of those first Japanese students, who looked desperately serious and determined.

Sakurai was born in 1858 in the Kaga domain; his childhood name was Jōgorō. His father died when he was five and he lived in poverty with his mother and elder brothers. At the age of 12, Sakurai started learning English from an Englishman, Percival Osborn, at an English-language school in Kanazawa. He went to Tokyo in 1871 and studied at Daigaku Nankō, which later became the Kaisei School, and specialised in chemistry. He changed his name to Jōji (George) while staying in Britain, since it was an easy name for English people to remember. Looking back on his time at UCL, he wrote:

> I studied at the University of London for five years. I was taught chemistry by Professor Williamson, and physics by Professor Foster and Dr Lodge. I also attended geology and mining engineering lectures. By sheer luck I passed the chemistry examination at the end of the first year with the best results and was awarded a gold medal [Fig. 32], and in the following year I passed the combined examination in chemistry and physics, again with the best results, and was awarded £100 (£50 a year for two years). The scholarship that I received from the government was 1,000 Mexican dollars a year and this was not quite enough, so the prize money was a great help for my research, and I still feel most grateful for the award. I did my research under Professor Williamson's guidance. I was not able to achieve a great deal but managed to publish two

Fig. 32   Gold medal awarded to Jōji Sakurai. Courtesy of National Museum of Nature and Science, Tokyo.

. short papers which I read at the Chemical Society of London and the British Association for the Advancement of Science. I was also elected as a member of the Chemical Society of London during my stay in Britain.[73]

Sir Oliver J. Lodge, the Dr Lodge mentioned by Sakurai above, was an assistant professor under Foster between 1879 and 1881, and then a professor at the University of Birmingham. Seven years before Sakurai's election to the Chemical Society of London, Kiyonari Yoshida, a former student from Satsuma, then visiting London as an under-secretary of the Ministry of Finance, had been elected a member on 25 July 1872. Williamson, Barff, Graham and Foster had taught Yoshida and they recommended him for membership. On the list of the Certificate of a Candidate for Election, Yoshida's position is marked as Vice-minister of Finance. He was sent to the United States and Britain to invite tenders for the purchase of Japanese government bonds with an interest rate of 0.7 per cent per annum.

A new document concerning Jōji Sakurai's time in Britain came to light in 2010. It is the transcript of a talk entitled 'The Ninth Year of Meiji: Memoir of my Time in Britain' and in it he described his time studying under Williamson:

I was in London between Meiji 9 and Meiji 14 [1877–82] and studied at London University. I went to London on the government's instruction to be trained in chemistry and I wanted to study under Professor Williamson who was not only the best (first-class) chemist in Britain but also widely known in the world. Professor Williamson had a long-standing link with Japan. At the end of the Edo Period, Count Itō, Count Inoue (Kaoru), Viscount Yamao and Viscount Inoue (Masaru) went to Britain, and they were kindly looked after by the professor. Viscount Inoue stayed with Professor Williamson's family for several years. Professor Williamson treated me with extreme kindness and I received immeasurable benefit through working under him. I received a strong influence from his great personality, and I owe all that I have managed to achieve to his guidance. I loved and respected him so much that I remained in London throughout my five years of study abroad without going elsewhere.[74]

This tells us that Sakurai intended to go to UCL from the beginning because he wanted to study under Williamson. He probably knew how Williamson had guided Chōshū students early on, and he had learned about Williamson's impressive research record from Atkinson and Masaki while at Tokyo Kaisei School.

Sakurai worked under Williamson's caring and excellent tutelage for four years and his research results were presented in August 1880 at the annual meeting of the British Association for the Advancement of Science in Swansea. The title of his paper was 'On Metallic Compounds Containing Bivalent Hydrocarbon-Radicals' and it won many people's attention. Sakurai had sent his manuscript to Williamson before the conference and received the following reply from him dated 20 August:

> My dear Sakurai
> I got home yesterday from Switzerland, where I have left my family to enjoy the mountains a little longer. I am glad to hear that you have continued to seek pleasure with improvement in the North and that you intend going to Swansea. I shall probably go down there on Tuesday. I have got the copy of your paper which you left for me and will give it to you when we meet there.
>   You ought to prepare a brief abstract of the paper to give to the Secretary of the Chemical Section when you read the paper.[75]

The historian of science Aiko Yamashita had high praise for Sakurai's research:

> He successfully obtained/synthesised the compounds $CH_2(HgI)_2$, $CH(HgI)_3$ and other derivatives. These compounds were important in structural chemistry, thus building on Williamson's embryonic

research on radicals. Sakurai's work set a precedent for further research on organo-metallic compounds in later years.[76]

There was another happy event for Williamson in 1880. One of his former students from Satsuma, Arinori Mori, returned to London after 15 years' absence and came to see him. After serving as the minister to China, and Vice-minister of Foreign Affairs in Tokyo, Mori became the Japanese minister in London in January 1880, accompanied by his family. On 4 February he was granted an audience with Queen Victoria, and while waiting to speak with her he unexpectedly met Benjamin Disraeli and took the opportunity to have a conversation with him. Disraeli, the leader of the Conservative Party, had a great interest in Asia and he welcomed the young minister from Japan. On the following day Mori attended, together with his wife Tsuneko, the opening ceremony of the House of Commons and met many diplomats.

The political situation

In 1880 Parliament had a stormy start. Disraeli's imperialist policies were facing a crisis. Since forming his second government in 1874, Disraeli had been actively involved in foreign policy. In 1875 Britain purchased a major interest in the Suez Canal Company, securing the route to the East. In 1876 Queen Victoria was proclaimed Empress of India, thus strengthening British control of the subcontinent. And in 1878 Britain prevented Russian advancement into the Balkans and obtained Cyprus. However, the Anglo-Zulu War in South Africa and the Second Anglo-Afghan War undermined public support for Disraeli and ultimately ended his political career. Taking advantage of Disraeli's failure, Gladstone successfully staged a comeback. In the general election of April 1880 the Liberals secured a large majority and Gladstone formed his second government. This signified the return of traditional Liberalism and the defeat of aggressive jingoism. However, the times did not allow Gladstone to remain a Liberal pacifist for long. To secure Britain's profit, he too had to shift to imperialistic policies. Imperialism had become unavoidable.

Arinori Mori

Six months after his arrival in London, Mori moved the Japanese consulate from 9 Kensington Park Gardens to 9 Cavendish Square.

The previous building was too small and it was time for Japan to find premises that fitted with the country's prestige. Japan had been working towards revision of the unequal treaties with America and European states. To achieve this aim, Mori needed to establish a diplomatic stronghold in London, since Britain was considered to be the biggest hurdle in the negotiations. The grand new building was originally an aristocrat's town house, and it remained standing there until the mid-1990s. It had a commanding position near the prestigious Langham Hotel to the northwest of the intersection of Regent Street with Oxford Street. It looked south onto Cavendish Square and east onto Chandos Street, which in turn leads to Portland Place. Slightly to the north, on Chandos Street, was the London Medical Association, with stables in its courtyard.

Based in the new consulate, Mori began his energetic diplomatic activity. In addition to his duties as a minister, he became a member of the Athenaeum Club in Pall Mall in order to broaden his knowledge and acquaintances, and to be involved in cultural activities. He was their first Japanese member. He used the opportunity to mix with British members, including Herbert Spencer, give presentations and hold dinners. Mori had not forgotten what he owed to Williamson. While he was in London he presented two large vases patterned with daisies. Emma cherished these gifts, which were later passed on to Williamson's son Oliver.

Mori also looked after the Japanese students who were in London, and Sakurai was often invited to the consulate in Cavendish Square. When Sakurai went back to Japan he left his photograph, signed 'With Jōji Sakurai's kind regards, London 17, vii 81', which is there in one of Mori's albums.

Britain as seen by Jōji Sakurai

Sakurai had a wonderful time in Britain. As well as working hard he thoroughly enjoyed himself, perhaps under Mori's influence. Reminiscing about those years, he wrote:

> Britain, during my time there, was experiencing a culturally glorious period under the reign of Queen Victoria. It felt as if Britain was in the vanguard of world culture, and there were so many distinguished people in so many fields of endeavour. I was probably a little intoxicated by the atmosphere. I started thinking that it was a shame, or perhaps even wrong, for me to spend all my time between laboratory and lodging house at such an exceptional

time … I managed to make good friends and they would often invite me to their homes. There were many opportunities to go out to dinners and balls, and I often danced until well after midnight, or even all night until morning. I am sure there were some who were critical of this kind of behaviour, but for me it was invaluable to realise that behind the grandeur of British culture stood a courteous and moderate people, and to experience their polite and convivial family lives.[77]

Sakurai learned to be a cultural relativist while in Britain, just as Mori did. He described his experience during this period using the expression 'cultural training', and refused to be an uncritical Anglophile. He became fully aware of the differences between British intellectuals and himself, a bearer of Japanese culture. Sakurai saw that his well-educated friends in Britain were very different from him in their politics, their scholarship, their manners and their family lives, and he tried to absorb only what he found good in British culture. This attitude and Williamson's 'unity out of difference' share common ground. Sakurai became known as a 'diplomat scientist' and his approach was of great advantage when it came to improving modern science education after his return to Japan.

Sakurai left London for Japan in July 1881. He visited the Williamsons at 15 Primrose Hill Road, where they had recently moved from their house in Fellows Road. He expressed his heartfelt gratitude to both Williamson and his wife Emma and presented them with a beautiful blue Japanese plaque which was also passed on to their son Oliver.

A pioneer Japanese chemist

On his return to Japan Sakurai was appointed as a junior lecturer of the Faculty of Science, Tokyo University. A few years before, on 20 October 1876, Yoshinari Hatakeyama had died prematurely at the age of 37 on a voyage across the Pacific. He had been the head of Tokyo Kaisei School and he was on his way back from seeing the World's Fair at Philadelphia. In April 1877 Tokyo Kaisei School was amalgamated with Tokyo Medical School to become Tokyo University. While Sakurai was still studying in Britain, Hiroyuki Katō, Professor of German, the university's first president, had arranged for him to come and teach at Tokyo University on his return, since it was vital that native Japanese scholars be employed.

A year later Sakurai was appointed as the first Japanese professor of chemistry at the tender age of 24, and during the next 38 years he was the most respected authority in the world of chemistry in Japan. He employed methods that he had learned from Williamson. At the beginning of his lectures, he explained: 'It is possible to master chemical analysis without the help of physics. But this kind of analysis is not the be-all and end-all of chemistry. Chemistry is the detailed research into the changes that occur with the movement of atoms.'[78]

Sakurai made a significant contribution by defining such technical terms as 'atom' and 'atomic weight', and producing fixed translations for them in Japanese. He wrote that the 'joy of being a scientist' was 'to advance world knowledge through research and to attain the honourable position of being a worker of the castle of knowledge. This is the true and highest honour and joy of a scientist.'[79]

Sakurai was proud of his country's culture of Noh plays. When Marie Stopes (1880–1958), a UCL graduate in geology and botany, visited Japan on a research fellowship in 1907 in order to search for fossilised plants in the coal mines of Hokkaido, Sakurai took her to performances. She became enchanted. Together, Stopes and Sakurai embarked on a project to make Noh plays known to Europeans. Their *Plays of Old Japan* (1910) was to influence the poetry of both W.B. Yeats and Ezra Pound.[80]

To digress a little: Kikunae Ikeda was the chemist who discovered the basis of the Japanese *umami* taste, *aji no moto* (monosodium glutamate). He was a student of Sakurai, and married Sakurai's younger sister. Sakurai's elder brother, Fusaki Sakurai, was the principal of Kumamoto No. 5 High School where the well-known writer Sōseki Natsume taught. It was perhaps Jōji Sakurai who introduced Sōseki Natsume to his former student Ikeda in London. They hit it off with each other, and shared lodgings for two months, discussing topics from literature to science. It is interesting to speculate that through Ikeda, Sōseki Natsume may have heard about Williamson.

High Pitfold House

In 1882 Williamson received two letters from Sakurai, one dated 4 January and the other 12 May, together with a third note on methylene compounds. He read the paper on behalf of Sakurai at the annual meeting of the Chemical Section of the British Science Association at Southampton. In his reply to Sakurai, dated 19 September, Williamson wrote, 'I need hardly tell you that it was very highly praised by various members of the Section' and added 'I am very much interested by your account of your work in Japan and feel sure that it will be of considerable value to your country … If any of your friends come over to England of course you will send them to me and I need not say that we shall receive them with the utmost pleasure.' At that time the Williamsons were enjoying their vacation in 'a pleasant neighbour-hood by Wellington College'; Williamson wrote, 'the soil about here is mere sand and of very little value for agriculture'. He also mentioned that 'One of the most remarkable social changes which has taken place since you left England has been the great development of the game of lawn tennis. My young people are very fond of it and never miss an opportunity of playing. There are so very few active outdoor games in which girls can take part that its introduction is really quite an important addition to their means of healthful exercise.'[81]

Williamson's letter suggested that his interests had shifted from pure academic research and the laws of science to the natural environment, including areas such as the human body and health, and he had probably already decided to move to a rural area. In 1885 Williamson sold land in Willesden, in northwest London, and bought an estate in High Pitfold near Haslemere in Surrey.

Haslemere is an old town in a valley 50 miles southwest of London close to the border with West Sussex. Nowadays it can be reached in less than an hour by train from Waterloo. At the time it was a thriving centre for artisanal products such as musical instruments, and beautiful old houses still line the streets to the present day. Its surrounding areas are wooded, and Tennyson, the poet laureate, is known to have composed poems on the small hill called Black Down to the south of the town. Shottermill, a beautiful scenic village along the River Wey, lies at the western end of the town. It had been part of Pitfold Manor and when the last owner, James Baker Jr, went bankrupt in 1881 several farms came on the market. Williamson bought a part of the former High Pitfold Farm, stretching over Portsmouth Road, and built a house, which he named High Pitfold House.

The house, representative of the time in which Williamson lived, was built in the Victorian Gothic style with red brick walls. The first-floor walls are imbricate and the two different brick layouts – normal layout for the ground floor and imbricate for the first – produced a wonderful effect. Together with the dark brown slate roof, the house still looks splendid.

Williamson seems to have particularly liked the bold assimilation of old and new elements that characterised Victorian architecture. Designers and artisans in London were involved in the Arts and Crafts movement under the banner of the 'unity of arts', defying the boundaries of visual arts. Many budding architects and young designers supported the movement, and William Morris and John Ruskin were core members. The first Arts and Crafts Exhibition opened in 1888 and gained popular support. Williamson might have seen the movement as reflecting his own idea of 'unity out of difference'. His newly built house was in the Victorian Gothic style and one could say that Williamson thereby gave the concept of 'unity out of difference' concrete shape. The house was surrounded by woodland, and horses and cows grazed peacefully in the nearby fields.

Williamson retired in 1887 after teaching at UCL for 38 years. He became Emeritus Professor of Chemistry and gave his retirement lecture on 'atomic motion', his favourite topic, on 14 June. His successor Sir William Ramsay, who was awarded the Nobel Prize in Chemistry in 1904, presided at the event. The Williamsons moved to High Pitfold House with new hopes. Their new life was not particularly easy but there was much to look forward to. Although Williamson had little knowledge of agriculture, he devoted himself to farming based on scientific principles. He was against Gladstone's policy of granting Home Rule to Ireland and campaigned against this with a neighbour, John Tyndall (1820–1893). Williamson seems to have got on well with Tyndall, a Professor of Natural Philosophy who had just retired as director of the Royal Institution in London. Williamson also became a member of the local council of Shottermill, and he was very much involved in projects to improve local people's living conditions, such as the creation of a working men's club.

Harmonising science and nature

Devoting himself to agricultural work, an unfamiliar occupation for him, in a beautiful natural environment, Williamson was, perhaps, attempting self-regeneration. He must have believed that harmony between modern science and the natural environment was the goal that modern civilisation should aspire to. He began to show signs of age after his seventieth birthday and journeys to London became somewhat difficult for him but he was undeterred, and went to London several times, including to a dinner for the former presidents of the Chemistry Society on 11 November 1898. In 1901 he fell and broke his left hand near Charing Cross Station and after this accident he lost some of his mobility.

On 22 January 1901 Queen Victoria died and Edward VII became king. The end of the Victorian era coincided with the end of the nineteenth century, an age of ground-breaking development in Western civilisation.

Williamson, who lived in and made many contributions to an age of progress and prosperity, felt the death of the queen deeply. That same year Williamson, who had become almost housebound, received the pleasant news that Sakurai was coming to England. Hearing this, Emma immediately sent a letter to Sakurai care of the Japanese consulate.

Twenty years had passed since Sakurai had left London and returned to Japan. He had become Professor of Chemistry at Tokyo Imperial University (renamed in 1886 by Arinori Mori, then the first Minister of Education), and was occupying a most prestigious position in the world of chemistry in Japan. According to Mori's 'Degree Ordinance' issued in 1887, Sakurai was awarded Japan's first doctorate in science. The purpose of Sakurai's trip in 1901 was to inspect educational institutions in Europe and America, and to attend a celebration to mark the four hundred and fiftieth anniversary of the University of Glasgow. He set sail from Yokohama on 3 May 1901 and arrived in Liverpool via the US on 6 June. On his arrival in London he went to see the minister, Tadasu Hayashi, at the Japanese consulate, which had by then moved to 4 Grosvenor Gardens, and delivered the medal of merit for Lord Kelvin (William Thomson) that he had brought from the Japanese government. Sakurai then visited Kelvin at his residence. He also met Edward Divers and expressed his deeply felt gratitude to him for his contribution to science education in Japan. Sakurai received Emma's letter at the consulate and was surprised to learn that Williamson had had an accident and had been seriously injured. He went to see the Williamsons at High Pitfold House the following day, 7 June. He left a vivid account of their emotional reunion:

> I was really shocked and worried when I heard that my former teacher Williamson, already at the advanced age of 77, had fallen and seriously injured himself. Receiving this news, I went to see him at his home in Haslemere the day after my arrival in London. Supported by his wife, Williamson kindly came to the door to meet me. With joy and indescribable feeling I was almost overwhelmed to see my old teacher and his wife, who were almost like my parents, after twenty years. He was also delighted to see me and hugged me tight; it was like a reunion of father and son. Fortunately he had recovered well, but I was sad to see that with his old age the accident had weakened him. His mind was completely clear and he talked fluently about things old and new just as before. He was particularly pleased with the remarkable developments Japan had made in the fields of politics, the economy, the military, academia and industry.

Professor Williamson looked after Duke Itō, Count Inoue and the late Viscount Mori[82] when they came to Britain for the first time. He helped them in many ways; finding language teachers, taking them to have clothes made, etc. I had already heard from Itō how kind he had been, and listening to Williamson talking about the old days I renewed my gratitude for his unfailing assistance towards us Japanese. The present minister, Viscount Hayashi, Baron Kikuchi and the late Masakazu Toyama were all taught by Professor Key, whose daughter is Williamson's wife. Many Japanese continued to be trained and guided by Professor Williamson, and we owe him a great deal for his assistance in the selection of suitable teaching staff from Britain when the first places of higher education for science, namely the former Kaisei School and the Civil Engineering College were created in Tokyo. He is a distinguished chemist who published new theories and it is universally acknowledged that he left a mark in the history of chemistry 50 years ago with his extraordinarily insightful views, and his extensive and important research.[83]

Sakurai here revealed his deep affection for his former teacher, and also described, in a concise way, what an important role Williamson had played in Japan's modernisation, and also his achievement as a chemist. This is a precious document that tells us something of Williamson's last years. The three students mentioned above, Tadasu Hayashi, Dairoku Kikuchi and Masakazu Toyama, were sent to Britain by the *bakufu* in January 1867, and they studied English at University College School where Emma's father, Professor Thomas Hewitt Key, was headmaster until 1875.

The spirit of 'unity out of difference'

We know from Sakurai's account that Williamson maintained a lively interest in all aspects of Japan's modernisation. He who had lived with the ideal of 'unity out of difference' must have found great joy in seeing that through Sakurai's work, Britain's modern chemistry and Western science had been properly transplanted to Japan. This meant to him the fusion of British and Japanese cultures.

Williamson took a keen interest in the work of all these pioneers in the development of modern Japan. Most of them kept up a regular

Fig. 33 Silver incense burner in lion shape made by Joun Ōshima. Courtesy of Sally-Anne Lenton.

correspondence with him and Mrs Williamson which lasted until the end of their lives, and even continued into the next generation. The letters from Japan contain expressions of deepest gratitude, indeed of veneration, to Williamson for his early teaching and beneficent influence.[84]

Williamson's interests were not limited to matters related to chemistry, and he paid attention to the ways in which his former students made contributions to their country. He read their letters carefully and replied to them with encouragement and appropriate advice. Whenever they came back to Britain, his students visited him with gifts. In Emma's will the following items were listed, in addition to those mentioned already.

From:
Hirobumi Itō   Two large Satsuma vases
                Two large bronze vases
                Incense burner in lion shape (from Mrs Itō to
                Mrs Williamson) [Fig. 33]
                White embroidered silk dolman and scarlet silk
                shawl (to Mrs Williamson)
                A coffee-coloured (pale) Japanese shawl (to
                Mrs Williamson)

Masaru Inoue	A Japanese fan (to Mrs Williamson, when he visited in 1910)
	Set of cloisonné ware
	A Japanese bag
	Japanese doll in case
Kiyonari Yoshida	Decorated box of lacquer ware with pearl inlay
	Japanese porcelain tea cups and plates
Jōji Sakurai	Japanese table cloth embroidered with chrysanthemum and butterflies and
	A Japanese table centre

Also 'a long Japanese letter box' that was believed to have once been in the possession of the Emperor was presented to Williamson. His former students sent him and his wife Emma many gifts to express their deep gratitude.

What Williamson had always tried to teach the young students from Japan was 'the spirit of studying science for its own sake'. Sakurai considered that he should be a bridge between Williamson and Japanese scientists who would come after him. So, in 1916, Sakurai, together with the chemist Jōkichi Takamine (1854–1922), who isolated and purified the hormone adrenaline, and the well-known industrialist Eiichi Shibusawa (1840–1931), founded Riken, a research institute, now Japan's largest comprehensive research institution. They also worked towards the establishment of the Japan Society for the Promotion of Science, which was founded in 1931.

Williamson firmly believed in true cultural fusion, and considered that 'unity out of difference' was possible if the spirit of Western science could be implanted in Japan. 'Of no one was he a keener critic than of himself',[85] and he never forgot the responsibilities of someone who represented science. He was thoughtful, earnest and broad-minded, and he always respected truth. Having met Sakurai for the last time after so many years, Williamson must have felt certain that his mission had been successfully handed on to his former student. On 6 May 1904 Williamson died peacefully in High Pitfold House, surrounded by his family. He.had just turned 80.

His body was buried a week later, on 13 May, on the south side of Brookwood Cemetery, close to the resting places of the four Japanese students who had died over 40 years ago. This must have been in accordance with his wishes. The funeral was organised by his son Oliver, of 55 Upper Berkeley Street, Portman Square.

Mrs Williamson died at the age of 92 at 147 Dartmouth Road, Brondesbury, almost 20 years later, on 27 September 1923. She left detailed instructions (dated 7 March 1913 and 1 July 1923) on how her personal belongings should be distributed. In her will she expressed her wish to be buried, either in a coffin or in a basket, in the grave of her husband, and also asked that her funeral be modest and simple. This is testimony to Emma's love and trust of her husband. She was buried on 1 October.

The Williamsons' simple grave, with their names, and dates of birth and death in small letters, stands in a corner of the Brookwood Cemetery (Fig. 34, Fig. 35).

Fig. 34 Gravestone of Alexander and Emma Williamson in Brookwood Cemetery. Courtesy of Nobutaka Sato.

Fig. 35 Black granite monument to Alexander and Emma Williamson. Courtesy of Nobutaka Sato.

Appendix
The names of the Chōshū Five and Satsuma Nineteen

The Chōshū Five

Kinsuke Endō (1836–1893)
Kaoru Inoue [aka Bunta Shiji] (1836–1915)
Masaru Inoue [aka Yakichi Nomura] (1843–1910)
Hirobumi Itō [aka Shunsuke Itō] (1841–1909)
Yōzō Yamao (1837–1917)

The students and accompanying officers from Satsuma

Supervising officers:
Tomoatsu Godai (1836–1885)
Takayuki Hori (1844–1911)
Hisanobu Niiro (1832–1889)
Munenori Terashima [aka Kōan Matsuki] (1832–1893)

Students:
Yoshinari Hatakeyama (1842–1876)
Hisanari Machida (1838–1897)
Seizō Machida (1851–1925)
Shinshirō Machida (1848–1910)
Junzō Matsumura [aka Kanjūrō Ichiki] (1842–1919)
Arinori Mori (1847–1889)
Hisanari Murahashi (1842–1892)
Kanae Nagasawa [aka Hikosuke Isonaga] (1852–1934)
Hiroyasu Nakamura (1844–1902)

Tokinari Nagoya (1847–1912)
Naonobu Sameshima (1845–1880)
Yaichi Takami (1831–1896)
Seishū Tanaka [aka Moriaki Asakura] (1843–1924)
Ainoshin Tōgō (1840?–1868)
Kiyonari Yoshida (1845–1891)

Epilogue and Acknowledgements

Shōgyō-ji, a Shin Buddhist temple near Tenman-gū Shrine in Dazaifu, houses a rare group of Japan's ancient traditional Gagaku music players called Chikushi Gakuso, and the sound of harmony the group produces is much appreciated, together with the Buddhist teaching of the Triratna.

In this temple, on 29 January 2012, a small gathering was organised to commemorate Professor Alexander William Williamson and his wife Emma. One of Williamson's pupils, Jōji Sakurai, the first chemistry professor of the Imperial University of Tokyo, once said that Williamson's contribution to the development of modern Japan was immense and that what we owe him is immeasurable. However, Williamson is completely forgotten in present-day Japan and the gathering was organised with the idea that it would be proper to express deeply felt gratitude to Williamson and his wife, who guided and looked after early Japanese travellers as if they had been their family members. Many people with links to Professor Williamson and also those involved in Anglo-Japanese associations travelled from Tokyo, Fukuoka, Yamaguchi, Saga, Kagoshima and many other places, responding to calls from the Head Priest of Shogyoji Temple, Venerable Chimyo Takehara, among them the former Vice-Provost of UCL, Professor John White, and Reverend Professor Kemmyo Taira Satō, a Visiting Professor of UCL and Director of Three Wheels, the London branch of Shōgyō-ji.

In today's world with all its disputes and conflicts, isn't it an apt time for the Japanese to renew our appreciation for the work and contribution of the British chemist who held the ideal of 'unity out of difference' throughout his life?

At the 2012 gathering it was decided to construct a monument commemorating the Williamsons in the Brookwood Cemetery in Britain, and to publish a biography. The Williamson monument, designed by Professor White, was completed in May 2013. The splendid unveiling ceremony took place at the cemetery on 2 July attended by Professor Malcolm Grant, the President and Provost of UCL, Dr Robert Parker, the

Chief Executive Officer of the Royal Society of Chemistry, and many other distinguished guests from Britain and other countries. Mr Keiichi Hayashi, Japan's Ambassador to the United Kingdom, unveiled the monument, and a letter of gratitude for the work of Professor Williamson and his wife from Prime Minister Shinzō Abe was handed to Professor Grant. After the ceremony, flowers were put on the Williamsons' grave and Chikushi Gakuso performed traditional Japanese music. Its solemn sound echoed throughout the cemetery as if it celebrated Williamson's spirit of harmony.

The year 2013 also marked 150 years since the first young men from Chōshū arrived in Britain to study. On 3 July a ceremony was held in front of the memorial stone at UCL. This monument, which had been created 20 years before and unveiled on 2 September 1993, celebrated the achievement of 24 students from Chōshū and Satsuma. Professor White, with whom the idea originated, designed it and supervised its construction in Portugal, instructing a Portuguese master craftsman in the principles underlying the carving of the very highest quality of extremely delicate *kanji* on its front face. I, for my part, decided which of the many possible variants of the students' names were to be used and drew the instructions in the particular type of historic *kanji* which I thought best suited for the actual carving of the monument. On the right hand side of the stone is engraved a *haiku* by Professor White:

When distant minds
come together
cherries blossom.

It expresses the feeling that people's minds communicate irrespective of national boundaries, and flowers bloom. When Professor White explained the meaning of this *haiku*, I felt that I could see the traditional spirit of UCL fostered for many years, and that this spirit no doubt shares something in common with Williamson's philosophy, 'unity out of difference'.

The plan to produce Williamson's biography progressed smoothly. Professor John White and Reverend Kemmyo Satō took on earnestly the task of gathering materials, and they found some new documents that had been unknown to researchers in Britain.

Reverend Keimei Takehara of Shōgyō-ji, Reverend Emmyo Satō who edited the book, Mr Yōsuke Yonemochi, designer of the book, and Mr Nobutaka Satō, a photographer, all came to Britain at various points. They examined the collected materials, visited many sites related to Williamson's life, and took many precious photographs.

The preparation was thorough. All necessary materials were gathered together and on-the-ground research for the biography was done. After that, I started writing in early summer 2014, and it was in December 2014 that I put my pen down. This year, 2015, marks 150 years since the 19 students from Satsuma travelled to Britain. I feel relieved, together with the feeling of the weight of responsibility, to have completed my work in time for publication to mark this important anniversary.

What I attempted in this book was to describe straightforwardly how Professor Williamson lived, and his personality, within the context of the time. As mentioned in the preface, the key concept is 'unity out of difference'. Placing Williamson at the central axis and putting those around him and the Japanese students under him in concentric zones, I tried to show how the modernisation of Japan progressed. Hence the subtitle: 'A Victorian chemist and the making of modern Japan'.

Many photographs, obviously shots by a professional photographer, appearing in the book do more than supplement my humble writing. I would be very happy if readers get a feeling for the time of Williamson's life and its atmosphere, through text and photographs.

I received support and help from many people, and this book could not have been completed without it. Venerable Chimyo Takehara and Mr Izumi Ida, Chairman of the Professor and Mrs Williamson's Monument Committee, made all the necessary arrangements for publication. I am most grateful to them. Professor White and Reverend Kemmyo Satō investigated and gathered materials concerned with Williamson's life and work and, thanks to them, it became possible to consult some materials at UCL that are not usually available to the public. Reverend Kemmyo Satō further investigated all the locations where Williamson lived and also managed to make contact with some of Williamson's descendants. I was so pleased to hear the news that they still possessed some of the things the Williamsons had left behind. I would like to express my deep gratitude for their assistance as it would not have been possible to write this book without these materials.

Mr John Fison, a great-grandson of the Williamsons, provided us with a family tree and family photographs including one of Mrs Emma Catherine Williamson. Mr Anthony Barr, the husband of the late Mrs Phoebe Barr, a great-granddaughter of the Williamsons, showed much understanding for our project and very kindly made the precious family collection, including the family's old album, available to us. Mrs Sally-Anne Fison Lenton, a great-great-granddaughter, provided us with Professor Williamson's royal medal and the silver lion incense burner given to Mrs Williamson by Mrs Hrobumi Itō. I am indebted to their kind generosity. It was my great joy to be able to welcome Mrs Lenton and her daughter Miss Amelia Rose Lenton to our meeting commemorating Professor Williamson held on 25 January 2015 at Shōgyō-ji. They were introduced to those who have been involved in producing this book. It was a great opportunity for me to be able to talk with them directly.

Professor Alwyn Davies gave us invaluable assistance in the area concerning Williamson's scientific papers, obituaries and related materials, and made those available to us. I received inspiring suggestions from Yoshiyuki Kikuchi, Associate Professor at the Graduate University for Advanced Studies in Japan. I learned from one of his papers that the method of chemistry teaching developed by Williamson and Charles Graham had a significant influence on the field of chemistry in Japan through Satsuma students and Jōji Sakurai. This information added to my motivation to write the book. I am grateful for Kikuchi's kind permission to translate excerpts from his paper from English into Japanese.

I am also indebted to Professor Hideaki Nagase of the University of Oxford and his wife, Professor Gill Murphy of Cambridge University, for their valuable advice regarding matters in the field of chemistry.

It was necessary to have specialist knowledge to translate Williamson's papers, obituaries and biographies, and I received help from people in various fields. I would like to express my gratitude particularly to Reverend Kemmyo Satō, Ms Hiroko Satō, Ms Junko Ida, Ms Yoshiko Hatae and Ms Sanae Takehara. I revised and rephrased parts of their translations by referring to the original texts, and I am solely responsible for any errors in the book.

I am grateful to the following libraries, museums and other organisations for allowing all of us to consult and in some cases make copies of materials and photographs. So many staff members at those institutions helped with this that it is impossible to name them all but I thank them profusely. UCL; Royal Society of Chemistry; Birkbeck College, University of London; Wellcome Library, London; British Library; National Portrait Gallery, London; National Maritime Museum London; Bank of England; London Metropolitan Archives; Camden Local Studies and Archives; Kensington and Chelsea Local Studies; General Register Office; National Archives Public Record Office; Haslemere Library; East Sussex Record Office; Higgins Art Gallery and Museum, Bedford; Yokohama Archives of History; Yamaguchi Prefecture Archives; Hagi Museum; Kagoshima Public Library, Reimeikan; Kagoshima Prefectural Center for Historial Material; Satsuma Students Museum; JCII (Japan Camera Industry Institute) Camera Museum; Tokyo Tech Museum and Archives; Nagasaki

University Library; National Diet Library; National Museum of Nature and Science; Japan Mint; Saga Prefectural Museum; Tokyo Gas, Gas Museum.

Mrs Michaela Vieser, residing in Berlin, kindly provided us with precious photographs of Heidelberg University and Giessen's Institute of Physical Chemistry. I would like to express my sincere thanks to Mr Keishō Ishiguro of Ishiguro Collection Preservation Society who provided many old photographs of the Japanese students and other related people of the time.

I should like to express my warmest thanks to Reverend Emmyo Satō of Shōgyō-ji who supervised the overall production of the book including typing my handwritten manuscript, and proofreading and editing the Japanese edition, and to Mr Yōsuke Yonemochi and Mr Satoshi Monma who were responsible for the design of the Japanese edition. The book was born as a result of my numerous meetings and discussions with these three people and I feel that it expresses the soul of all four of us. I very much hope that readers enjoy turning page by page.

I thank Kaichōsha for their decision to publish the original edition of this book despite the difficult publishing circumstances of the present day.

I would like to dedicate the book to the spirits of Professor Alexander William Williamson and his wife Emma.

6 May 2015
The first day of summer by the old calendar

Takaaki Inuzuka

Afterword
Serendipity: The ever-widening circle

There can be no better illustration of the fact that we can never tell the consequences of the things we do than the story of Professor Alexander William Williamson. When he welcomed five young Japanese students into his department and his home in 1863, and took care of a further, larger wave of escapees in 1865, he can have had not the slightest inkling of what they would become.

To say that Hirobumi Itō was a four-time prime minister of Meiji Japan (1885–8, 1892–6, 1898 and finally 1900–1) gives almost no idea of what that actually means in this particular case, and Professor Takaaki Inuzuka in his epoch-making biography very wisely refrains from any attempt to turn it into some enormous *omnium gatherum*. There is therefore much that remains unsaid.

Certainly, Hirobumi Itō was the best known of what is now referred to as the Chōshū Five, and he was no mere figurehead. It was he himself who was personally responsible for the drafting of the Constitution of the revolutionary form of government which was sanctioned by the now powerful Emperor Meiji in February 1889, and swept away all vestiges of the medieval feudal system of the shogunate, a form of military dictatorship that had held sway in Japan from 1185 to 1868.

After travelling extensively in Europe and working in the US and observing other forms of government, the one he chose to follow, since it fitted in so well not only with his own conservative instincts but also with the previous history of Japan, was the Prusso-German model of an emperor with considerable powers and an elected imperial Diet, though with the latter taking a bicameral form resembling that in the US. Similarly, he could not possibly know how easily, and for what quite different purposes, what he had done could be modified by MacArthur in the wake of World War II.

During this same period of gestation, his lifelong close friend, Kaoru Inoue, who had from the first adopted the slogan of 'a strong military and a prosperous country', became successively Under-Secretary of State for Financial Affairs (1871–3), Secretary of State for Foreign Affairs and subsequently Minister of Foreign Affairs (1879–87), in which post he served in Hirobumi Itō's first cabinet.

Masaru Inoue, on the other hand, became in 1871 the first director of the Japanese Railways Board, supervising the construction of the Nakasendō Railway and playing a leading role in the proposals for future mainline railway networks, which have since become, with the mixture of high-speed Shinkansen lines and competing, humble local and commuting systems, certainly the finest in the world. He died in London during an official visit in 1910, and in 1984 his direct descendant, Katsuhide Inoue, established, in accordance with his wishes, a scholarship in his name at UCL to enable British students to study in Japan.

For Hirobumi Itō the returning of the emperor to power was not simply an action he saw as a political necessity. The very word implies the existence of an empire, which is often associated with the idea of conquest, but in its essence is the coming together or unification of number of disparate elements under a single ruler. For Itō the essential base was nationhood, which in Japan meant the replacement of clan loyalty to a feudal lord or *daimyō* with a new conception of themselves as Japanese, whose primary loyalty was to the person of the emperor as ruler of a nation.

This process, for the Chōshū and Satsuma students, started early on when several members of the two groups under Williamson's wing happened to meet each other for the first time. Quite quickly, as Professor Inuzuka shows, they quietly began to behave not as clan members, but as fellow Japanese in a strange new world.

Under Itō's leadership the idea of Japanese nationhood developed with extraordinary rapidity. It was during his second period as prime minister that the Sino-Japanese War of 1894–5 took place and resulted, in the Treaty of Shimonoseki of 1895, in Korea's being transferred from vassalage to China to being recognised as in the Japanese sphere of influence. Then, in the Russo-Japanese War of 1904–5, Japan became the first Asian nation to defeat a European power, and its new status as a major force in international power politics was epitomised by the fact that it was in New Hampshire in the US that President Theodore Roosevelt brokered the Treaty of Portsmouth, which recognised Japanese primacy in Korea.

But Itō was no simple knee-jerk imperialist and when, as governor general, he was assassinated in 1909 by a Korean independence activist, he was actively opposing those who wanted a straightforward annexation of Korea lock, stock and barrel.

Already in 1894, during Itō's second period as prime minister, the Anglo-Japanese Treaty of Commerce and Navigation had been signed, to be followed, only one year after his fourth term, by the Anglo-Japanese Treaty of Alliance directed against Russian expansion in the Far East.

No one could possibly have guessed what was already brewing in the short six months that Horobumi Itō and Kaoru Inoue had spent in London under Williamson's tutelage.

The name of Kinsuke Endō, another of the Chōshū Five, is little known in Britain to say the least, yet he has undoubtedly been a household name for the hundreds of thousands of Japanese who over the years have visited the famous Sakura Avenue of cherry trees that he planted in the grounds of the Mint, which was established in Osaka and of which he became the first director. The planting of cherry trees has nothing to do with chemistry or with Williamson himself, and most British people were and still are completely unaware of the cultural significance of the centuries-old traditions surrounding the annual cherry blossom viewing season in Japan. Yet if Endō had not come to Britain as a member of the Chōshū Five and been among the group who came together under Williamson, it is quite likely that he would never have become director of the Mint and the Sakura Avenue would not now exist.

When Yōzō Yamao went to work in the Glasgow shipyards in 1866 for purely military purposes, the circle of Williamson's influence once more widened in a wholly unexpected way. The education of deaf and dumb children in Japan quite naturally finds no place in this biography by Professor Inuzuka. But if Yamao, acting on Williamson's insistence on the absolute necessity of practical experience as well as theoretical knowledge, had not gone in 1866 to work in the Glasgow shipyards, to train himself for purely military purposes as an engineer, he himself would have been wholly unaware of what would follow for him for the rest of his life. Immediately he started work, he found that the noise in a nineteenth-century shipyard was so deafening that his new companions had to use sign language to communicate. The result was that as soon as he got back to Japan he devoted vast amounts of energy to creating the first schools in Tokyo for the education of the blind and of the deaf and dumb, which led to the transformation of their lives, a work in which successive members of his family have been leaders ever since. He himself quickly rose to be Secretary of State in the Ministry of Industries and was instrumental in creating the structural framework for Japan's technological revolution.

Even a cursory glance of the subsequent careers of the two waves of young Japanese who came under the influence of Williamson in 1863 and 1865 shows that in one way or another almost half of them reached the highest levels in the governance and politics of the new Japan and in the major industries associated with its rise. That time and again the circle of Williamson's influence widened in a totally unpredictable manner is also the case, as will be seen, with some of the Satsuma pioneers of 1865.

Munenori Terashima played an instrumental part in the founding of the Foreign Ministry of which he was for a time the Secretary of State. As a diplomat, as well as serving in London in 1872–3, in 1875 he negotiated the Treaty of St Petersburg which fixed the national boundaries between Russia and Japan, but ultimately failed, largely through British opposition, in his attempts to have the unequal treaties with the US, which had been signed under the shogunate, revised.

Naonobu Sameshima was Japanese envoy to France in 1878, and in 1880 Japanese minister in Portugal and Spain, while Hiroyasu Nakamura served in Russia, Holland and Denmark. Yoshinari Hatakeyama played an active role in the reform of the Japanese educational system and was the first head of the Tokyo Kaisei College, which later became the University of Tokyo. Hisanari Machida was the founder and in 1875 first head of what eventually became the Tokyo Imperial Museum, which was modelled on London's Victoria and Albert Museum. But then, in an unexpected turn of events, he suddenly gave up his post as Japan's first director of museums to become chief priest of Kōjōin Miidera Temple in Shiga prefecture.

In terms of serendipity, the story of Hisanari Murahashi is almost a carbon copy of this singular happening, since after distinguishing himself in the Imperial Army and serving in the Yezo Land Development Office, in which capacity he introduced Western agricultural technology to the area, he suddenly resigned to become a Buddhist monk.

There were no such unexpected events in the career of Junzō Matsumura, who simply kept throughout his life this, the assumed name he was given before embarking on the perilous escape to London, and after spending some time in the US, quietly rose to be the head of the Japanese Naval Academy.

Ainoshin Tōgō returned to Japan and in 1868 was among those killed in the Boshin Civil War, which ended the rule of the shogunate.

The career of Arinori Mori, who joined the expedition at the age of 17 and is one of the more familiar of the Satsuma students, is in some ways the most surprising. After quite soon going to the US, together with Naonobu Sameshima, Kiyonari Yoshida, Yoshinari Hatakeyama, Junzō Matsumura and Kanae Nagasawa, under the influence of Thomas Lake Harris, the leader of an American religious community, he returned to Japan in 1868 and became the first Minister of Education. He was primarily concerned with the improvement of the existing system, but his outspoken proposals for such things as the abolition of swords, and his declaration at one point that Japanese should be replaced by English, made him extremely unpopular in certain quarters. In 1889 he was assassinated by a Japanese nationalist.

Finally, I would like to end this briefest of summaries of the achievements of some of the Satsuma students of 1865, and the outcome of their period at UCL, by looking at two extremes: at Kanae Nagasawa and Tomoatsu Godai, neither of whose subsequent careers, for very different reasons, receive much mention in Professor Inuzuka's book, and yet both do much in their own way to throw light on the nature of the Satsuma expedition.

At one end of the spectrum is Kanae Nagasawa, who was born Hikosuke Isonaga, but kept to his assumed name for the rest of his life. He was at 13 far the youngest of those who took part in the Satsuma expedition and only spent two months in direct contact with Professor Williamson. His setting out on such an initially perilous journey is not only a tribute to his own bold and adventurous spirit, but also epitomises the easily forgotten determination and fortitude of the families that the students left behind. Despite his youth, he was the most accomplished English speaker of the whole of the Satsuma student group, but because he was too young to enter university, almost immediately after his arrival he left, as had already been agreed, to live in Aberdeen with the family of James, the younger brother of Thomas Glover of Jardine Matheson, whose ships had transported the two groups of Japanese students to London.

In Aberdeen he enrolled in the Gymnasium, a secondary school, and Professor Inuzuka records that Yamao, who had kept in touch, soon said that Glover had told him that Kanae was 'just like the other local boys', though that may not be quite true, as he actually came first, with excellent grades in Latin, English and geography.

Since, like many of the other students, he began to suffer from a lack of funds because of money not arriving from Japan, he joined the group that left for the USA in 1867, and was the only one to remain with Harris after the other five had left, and carried on the former's business.

He became in fact the first Japanese to settle permanently in the US, and achieved such great success in the winemaking business that he came to be known as 'the grape king of California'.

The story of Tomoatsu Godai could hardly be more different since, as Professor Inuzuka records, it was his proposal in 1864 that resulted, under his own leadership, in the Satsuma expedition of 1865. When he returned to Japan in 1866, he served in the Meiji government for a time as Junior Counsellor for Foreign Affairs, Assistant Judicial Officer of the Foreign Affairs Office and Osaka Prefectural Judge. Then, in 1869, he resigned and rapidly became the Japanese entrepreneurial equivalent of the innumerable British entrepreneurs who were continuing to turn their country into the world's first great industrial nation.

He swiftly rose to be a leading figure in the transformation of Osaka, where his statue stands, into the modern commercial centre which it now is in the form of Japan's third largest city after Tokyo and Yokohama. He established a foreign settlement and built the port offices, which still survive; was active in the founding of the National Mint Bureau and the Osaka Tax Office; and later on set up the chamber of commerce and industry and the stock exchange, as well as being active in mining, in the building of the Osaka to Kobe railroad and in the construction of some 350 steam locomotives.

Later in life Professor Williamson himself began to concern himself in a small way with commercial enterprises, but no one ever, among all the Japanese who studied under him, however briefly, took more thoroughly to heart his early and lifelong insistence on the linkage between theoretical knowledge and commercial and industrial practice than did Tomoatsu Godai.

John White

Fig. 36 Memorial at UCL erected in 1993 to mark the 130th anniversary of the visit of the Chōshū Five. Courtesy of Nobutaka Sato.

Further reading

Brock, W.H. 1981. 'The Japanese Connexion: Engineering in Tokyo, London and Glasgow', *British Journal History of Science* 14: 227–43.

Brock, W.H. 2004. 'Alexander William Williamson', in Bernard Lightman, ed., *The Dictionary of Nineteenth-Century British Scientists*, vol. 4. Bristol: Continuum, 3168–75.

Checkland, Olive. 1989. *Britain's Encounter with Meiji Japan, 1868–1912*. Basingstoke: Macmillan.

Clark, Robin J.H. and Mitsuo Tasumi. 1984. 'Sakurai, Japanese Chemistry, and University College London', *Chemistry in Britain* 20: 1000–1.

Cobbing, Andrew. 1998. *The Japanese Discovery of Victorian Britain: Early Travel Encounters*. Richmond: Japan Library.

Cobbing, Andrew and Takaaki Inuzuka. 2000. *The Satsuma Students in Britain*. Richmond: Japan Library.

Davies, Alwyn and Peter Garrett. 2013. *UCL Chemistry Department 1828–1974*. St Albans: Science Reviews 2000.

Davies, Alwyn. 2015. 'Alexander Williamson and the Modernisation of Japan', *Science Progress* 98(3): 276–90.

Divers, Edward. 1907. 'Alexander W. Williamson', *Proceedings of the Royal Society* 78A: xxix–xliv.

Foster, G. Carey. 1905. 'Alexander William Williamson', *Journal of the Chemical Society* 87: 605–18.

Harris, J. and W.H. Brock. 1974. 'From Giessen to Gower Street: Towards a Biography of Alexander William Williamson (1824–1904)', *Annals of Science* 31: 95–130.

Kikuchi, Yoshiyuki. 2013. *Anglo-American Connections in Japanese Chemistry: The Lab as Contact Zone*. New York: Palgrave Macmillan.

Paul, E. Robert. 1978. 'Alexander W. Williamson on the Atomic Theory', *Annals of Science* 35: 17–31.

Rocke, Alan J. 1993. *The Quiet Revolution: Hermann Kolbe and the Science of Organic Chemistry*. Berkeley: University of California Press, chapter 6.

Rocke, Alan J. 2004. 'Alexander William Williamson', *Oxford Dictionary of National Biography*.

Notes

1 Foster, G.C. 1905. 'Alexander William Williamson: Obituary', *Journal of the Chemical Society* 87: 605–18.
2 Harris, J. and W.H. Brock. 1974. 'From Giessen to Gower Street: Towards a Biography of Alexander William Williamson (1824–1904)', *Annals of Science* 31(2): 95–130.
3 Harris and Brock, 'From Giessen to Gower Street', 101.
4 Harris and Brock, 'From Giessen to Gower Street', 101; Stumm, Petra. 2012. *Leopold Gmelin (1788–1853): Leben und Werk eines Heidelberger Chemikers.* Freiburg: Centaurus.
5 Brock, W.H. 1997. *Justus von Liebig: The Chemical Gatekeeper.* Cambridge: Cambridge University Press.
6 Divers, Edward. 1907. Obituary of Williamson, *Proceedings Royal Society* 78A: xxiv–xliv, at p. xxvi.
7 The degree was awarded to Williamson for his paper entitled 'Über die Zersetzung einiger Metalloxyde und Salze durch Chlor' (On the decomposition of some metal oxides and salts by chlorine).
8 Harris and Brock, 'From Giessen to Gower Street', 105.
9 Harris and Brock, 'From Giessen to Gower Street', 106.
10 Foster, 'Alexander William Williamson'.
11 Harris and Brock, 'From Giessen to Gower Street', 108.
12 Foster, 'Alexander William Williamson'.
13 Harris and Brock, 'From Giessen to Gower Street', 107.
14 Letter from Alexander W. Williamson to the Council of University College. Paris, 26 April 1849. UCL Special Collections, UCLCA/CORR/2911.
15 Testimonial by Dr Justus Liebig on behalf of the Council of University College. Giessen, 1 May 1849. UCL Special Collections, UCLCA/CORR/2911.
16 Letter from Alexander W. Williamson to Charles C. Atkinson. London, 25 June 1849. UCL Special Collections, UCLCA/CORR/2911.
17 Russell, Colin. 2004. 'Ethereal Philosopher', *Chemistry World*, https://www.chemistryworld.com/features/ethereal-philosopher/3004583.article, last accessed 18 August 2020.
18 Harris and Brock, 'From Giessen to Gower Street', 110.
19 Foster, 'Alexander William Williamson: Obituary', 610.
20 Hirota, J. 2013. *Gendai kagaku shi – genshi to bunshi no kagaku no hatten.* Kyoto: Kyoto daigaku gakujutsu shuppan kai.
21 Briggs, Asa. 1954. *Victorian People: Some Reassessments of People, Institutions, Ideas and Events, 1851–1867.* London: Odhams Press, 16.
22 University College School was at that time within the grounds of UCL.
23 Bellot, H.H. 1929. *University College London 1826–1926.* London: University of London Press, 92.
24 Bellot, *University College London 1826–1926*, 89.
25 Harris and Brock, 'From Giessen to Gower Street', 114.
26 Harris and Brock, 'From Giessen to Gower Street', 122.
27 Harris and Brock, 'From Giessen to Gower Street', 115.
28 Williamson, A.W. 1865. *Chemistry for Students.* Oxford: Clarendon Press, Preface.
29 Suematsu, K., ed. 1911–20. *Bōchō kaiten shi*, vol. 4, 169–70. Tokyo: Matsuno Shoten.
30 *North China Herald*, 4 July 1863.
31 Shunpokō Tsuishōkai, ed. 1940. *Itō Hirobumi den*, vol. 1. Tokyo: Harashobō, 105.

32 Nakahara, K. 1907. *Inoue Haku den*, vol. 2. Tokyo: K. Nakahara.
33 Dykes, J.O. 1899. *Memorials of Hugh M. Matheson*. London: Hodder & Stoughton, 104.
34 Foster, 'Alexander William Williamson: Obituary', 617.
35 Foster, 'Alexander William Williamson: Obituary', 617.
36 Originally edited by Tsumagi Chūta and published by Hayakawa Ryōkichi in 1932–3. Reprinted in Nihon Shiseki Kyōkai, ed. 1985. *Kido Takayoshi nikki*, vol. 2. Tokyo: Tokyo Daigaku Shuppankai.
37 Suematsu, K. 1900. *Ishin Fūunroku: Itō, Inoue ni-genrō jikiwa*. Tokyo: Tetsugaku Shoin.
38 Harris and Brock, 'From Giessen to Gower Street', 123.
39 Williamson, A.W. 'Development of Difference The Basis of Unity: Introductory Lecture to the Courses of the Faculty of Arts and Laws, University College, London', lecture delivered 16 October 1849.
40 Inoue, K. 1901. 'Kaikyū dan' in *Bōchō Shidankai zasshi*, 17–19.
41 Itō, H. 1936. *Itō kō jikiwa*. Tokyo: Chikura shobō.
42 Reginald Russell, 'Memorandum. Japan', National Archives, Kew, FO 46/49, 1 July 1864.
43 Russell, 'Memorandum. Japan'.
44 Having been released by the British, Godai had to go into hiding because leaving the domain without permission was a serious offence.
45 Inuzuka, T. and H. Uenuma, eds. 1999. 'Matsumura Junzō's Diary', *Shinshū Mori Arinori zenshū*, vol. 4. Tokyo: Bunsendō Shoten.
46 Inuzuka and Uenuma, eds. 1999. 'Hatakeyama Yoshinari's Diary', *Shinshū Mori Arinori zenshū*, vol. 4.
47 Inuzuka and Uenuma, eds. 1999. 'Hatakeyama Yoshinari's Diary', *Shinshū Mori Arinori zenshū*, vol.4.
48 Inuzuka and Uenuma, eds. 1999. 'Machida Hisanari's Diary', *Shinshū Mori Arinori zenshū*, vol. 4.
49 UCL Special Collections, UCLCA/CORR/2911.
50 Kagoshima-ken Rekishi Shiryō Sentā Reimeikan. 1995. *Kagoshima-ken shiryō Tamazato Shimazu-ke shiryō* 4. Kagoshima. Niiro's report was dated 16 September 1865.
51 Dykes, *Memorials of Hugh M. Matheson*, 105.
52 Kido Takayoshi Kankei Bunsho Kenkyūkai, ed. 2005. 'Ito Hirobumi's Letter to Kido Takayoshi', *Kido Takayoshi kankei bunsho*, vol. 1. Tokyo: Tokyo Daigaku Shuppankai, 225.
53 *London and China Express*, 10 March 1866.
54 Shunpokō Tsuishōkai, *Itō Hirobumi den*, vol. 1, 677.
55 Inuzuka, T. and H. Uenuma, eds. 1999. *Shinshū Mori Arinori zenshū*, vol. 3. Tokyo: Bunsendō Shoten, 49.
56 Inuzuka and Uenuma, *Shinshū Mori Arinori zenshū*, vol. 3, 56.
57 Bright, J. 1930. *The Diaries of John Bright*. London: Cassell, 305.
58 Habusa, Y. 1929. *Ikyō gaiyūki*. Hanabusa Tarō.
59 Kōshaku Shimazu-ke Hensanjo, ed. 1968. *Sappan kaigun shi*, vol. 2. Tokyo: Hara shobō, 980.
60 Kido Takayoshi Kankei Bunsho Kenkyūkai, ed. 2005. *Kido Takayoshi bunsho*, vol. 2. Tokyo: Tokyo Daigaku Shuppankai.
61 Kido Takayoshi Kankei Bunsho Kenkyūkai, *Kido Takayoshi bunsho*, vol. 1.
62 Williamson, A.W. 1869. 'On the Atomic Theory', *Journal of the Chemical Society* 22: 328–65 at 365.
63 Williamson, A.W. 1870. *A Plea for Pure Science: Being the Inaugural Lecture at the Opening of the Faculty of Science, University College London*. London: Taylor and Francis.
64 Williamson, *A Plea for Pure Science*, 20.
65 Williamson, *A Plea for Pure Science*, 26.
66 Stevenson, R.L. 1880. 'Yoshida-Torajiro', repr. in *Works of Robert Louis Stevenson*, vol. 5, 1895. London: Chatto & Windus, 173.
67 Iwakawa, T. 1926. 'Mōrusu sensei o tsuitōsu', *Dōbutsugaku zasshi* 38: 453.
68 Williamson, A.W. *Chemistry for Students*, third edition. Oxford: Clarendon Press, 1873.
69 Sakurai, J. 1924. 'Meiji Jidai no Kagaku', in *Meiji bunka hasshō kinen shi*. Tokyo: Dai Nihon Bunmei Kyōkai.
70 Ueno, M. 1968. *Oyatoi gaikokujin 3: Shizen Kagaku*. Tokyo: Kajima Kenkyūjo Shuppankai.
71 Sakurai, J. 1940. *Omoide no kazukazu*. Tokyo: Kyūwakai.
72 Bellot, *University College London 1826–1926*.
73 Sakurai, *Omoide no kazukazu*.

74   Ishii, S. 2011. 'Sakurai Jōji no "Meiji kyūnen eikoku ryūgaku no kaikyūdan"', *Nihon Gakushiin kiyō* 66(1).
75   Quoted in Kikuchi, Y. 2004. 'Sakurai Joji to igirisujin kagakusha konekushon', *Kagakushi kenkyu* 31(4), 239–67.
76   Yamashita, A. 1963. 'Reimeiki Nippon ni kagaku no kiso o kizuita Sakurai Jōji – oyobi kare o meguru hitobito', *MOL Kagaku gijutsu shi* 4(6).
77   Sakurai, *Omoide no kazukazu*.
78   Yamashita, 'Reimeiki Nippon ni Kagaku no kiso o kizuita Sakurai Jōji – oyobi kare o meguru hitobito'.
79   Sakurai, J. 1888. 'Rigakusha no kairaku', *Tōyō gakugei zasshi* 84.
80   Stopes, Marie C. and J. Sakurai. 1910. *Plays of Old Japan*; Stopes and Sakurai. 1927. *Plays of Old Japan. The Nō*. See also Stopes, Marie C. (1910) *Journal from Japan*.
81   Quoted in Kikuchi, 'Sakurai Jōji to Igirisujin kagakusha konekushon', *Kagakushi kenkyū* 31 (4), 258.
82   Mori Arinori was assassinated in February 1889.
83   Sakurai, J. 1902. 'Ōbei junkai zakki', *Tōyō gakugei zasshi* 19: 249.
84   Harris and Brock, 'From Giessen to Gower Street', 125.
85   'Obituary Notices of Fellows Deceased', *Proceedings of the Royal Society A* 78(526): xliv.

Index

CPSIA information can be obtained
at www.ICGtesting.com
Printed in the USA
BVHW020728291021
619880BV00041B/358